The 500 Hidden Secrets of

LONDON

D1340983

INTRODUCTION

This book invites you to leave the beaten track and to explore unknown and surprising places in London. The main objective of this publication is to guide the reader to the places that are not usually included in tourist guides. Like the outdoor pool with an award-winning cafe, or the peaceful garden found in the ruins of a City church, or the Turkish pool hall that hosts club nights and indoor golf. At the same time it also lists fantastic places to discover and buy contemporary crafts, the finest specialist bookstores and many other places, cafes, galleries and shops that represent the best that London has to offer. It also includes some unusual experiences, like mudlarking on the shore of the Thames for Roman coins or swimming in a natural pool amongst a land art project in King's Cross.

The guide reflects the huge changes that have occurred in the city over the past decade or so. There has been a significant shift eastwards in the centre of gravity of the city's population, enterprise, culture and hipness. Hackney and east London have emerged as some of the most exciting areas to live, work and play in. The addresses chosen are indicative of this, but at the same time feature the most compelling attractions on offer in all parts of the city.

Finally this guide does not mention everything you can see and do in London. Rather, the aim of this guide is to be intimate, personal and to offer surprising insights that are based on experience. The author shares his favourite places with his readers, much as he would do with a friend who was visiting London.

HOW TO USE
THIS BOOK?

———

This guide lists 500 places to go to in London or things to know about the city. There are 100 different categories, with 5 places each. Most of these are places to visit – restaurants, cafes, pubs, shops, galleries, museums or streets and parks. We have included practical information like the address, the phone number and the website where these are available.

For the purpose of this guide London has been divided into 15 districts, each with its own map that can be found at the beginning of the book. Each address is numbered from 1 to 500 and the district and map number are detailed in the description. This will help you to locate the address on the maps. A word of caution however: due to the large geographic area covered in the guide these maps are not always detailed enough to allow you to locate specific locations in the city. A good map can be obtained from any tourist information centre or from most good hotels. Or the addresses can be located on a smartphone.

The author also wishes to emphasise that a city like London constantly changes. So a delicious meal at a restaurant may not taste quite as good on the day you visit it. Ownership and staffing of an address may change and with it the quality of service and experience. This personal and subjective selection is based on the author's experience, at the time this guide was compiled. If you want to add a comment, suggest a correction, recommend a place or share your own secret place in London with us then contact the editor at *info@lusterweb.com*. Or follow *@500hiddensecrets* on Instagram and leave a comment – you'll also find free tips and the latest news about the series there.

THE AUTHOR

Tom Greig has lived and worked in London for nearly 15 years. His work as a sales representative for art publishers takes him to every part of the city – to bookshops, galleries, museums, institutions, concept stores and design outlets. Endlessly curious about his city and its secrets, culture and history, he takes every opportunity to make new discoveries on his travels across London's many districts. He's always alert to the possibility of finding a newly opened shop, a better spot for coffee or an interesting building or green space that's waiting to be discovered off the main drag.

A music lover, record collector and DJ (www.mixcloud.com/tom-greig/), he is also an avid cyclist, enthusiastic outdoor swimmer, coffee drinker and pub aficionado. According to Tom it is impossible even for seasoned Londoners to truly know all aspects of the city, such is its geographic scale and the breadth of attractions and experiences it offers. Furthermore, it is in a constant state of flux and change that is almost impossible to keep up with. Trying to pin it down definitively is futile, which is why this guide is so useful in pointing the reader towards a few interesting and friendly starting points for making their own discoveries.

The author wishes to thank the many people who have helped him to draw up the list of 500 special places. Friends, family, colleagues and acquaintances have proved invaluable in providing tips and advice, and for their willingness to champion their own favourite secret spots. In particular, he is grateful to Alex Madden for his *bon vivant's* knowledge of places to eat and drink, to Nadine Hawkins for her fashion expertise, to

Hackney *habitué* Cantlin Ashrowan, and finally to Louisa, who for a while lost her husband during the completion of this project, for introducing him to many of these places.

He would also like to thank photographer Sam Mellish for his dedication to the project and for the wonderful images that have captured London's vital essence so well. At Luster, he thanks Tania Van de Vondel for so readily taking up the suggestion of a London entry in the 500 Hidden Secrets series, and Dettie Luyten for happily steering the book to completion. Thanks also go to Sudha d'Unienville and James Smith for taking him out of London's bookshops and onto its streets.

LONDON

overview

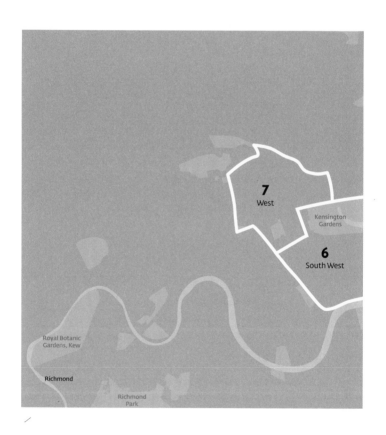

7
West

Kensington
Gardens

6
South West

Royal Botanic
Gardens, Kew

Richmond

Richmond
Park

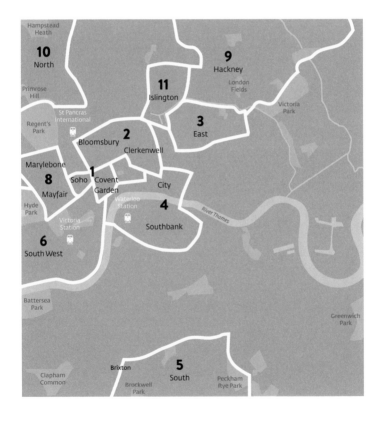

Map 1
SOHO

COVENT GARDEN

Map 2
BLOOMSBURY

↑ 349

119

250

St Pancras
International
Station

Grays Inn Rd

264

Euston Rd

Euston
Station

141

Euston Rd

122

Regent Square

Tavistock Square

Tavistock Pl

Marchmont St

Brunswick Square

Cower St

482

Gordon Square

Woburn Pl

320

Guilford St

160

74

Russel
Square

Queen Square

117

229

Southampton Row

377

Tottenham Court Rd

412

Russell Square

Bedford Square

Bloomsbury St

The British
Museum

230

201

Lambs Conduit St

232

319

Oxford St

156

CLERKENWELL

Map 3
EAST

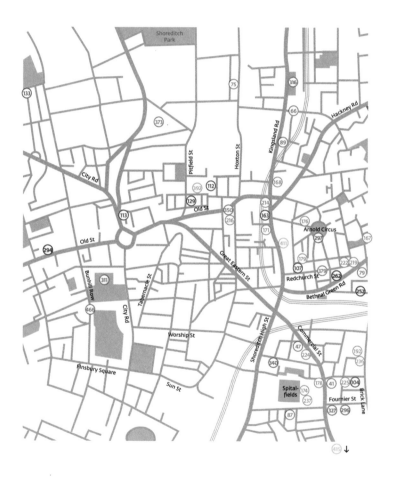

Map 4
CITY *and* SOUTHBANK

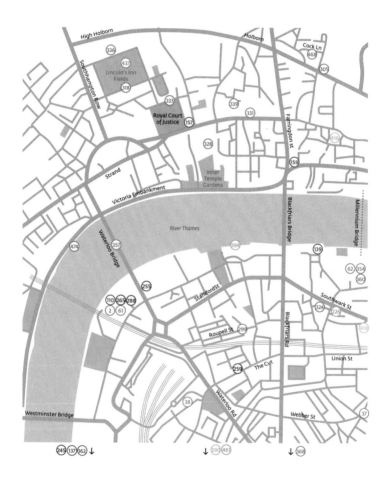

High Holborn
Holborn
Cock Ln
468
336
305
437
Lincoln's Inn
Fields
318
333
339
331
Southampton Row
Royal Court
of Justice 157
Farringdon St
328
416
Strand
159
Inner
Temple
Gardens
Victoria Embankment
River Thames
Blackfriars Bridge
Millennium Bridge
474
157
Waterloo Bridge
394
139
255
62 354
360
110 265 288
Stamford St
2 61
Southwark St
324
226
Roupell St
299
418
Blackfriars Rd
259
The Cut
Union St
38
Waterloo Rd
249 137 162 ↓
↓ 390 461
Webber St
37
↓ 368

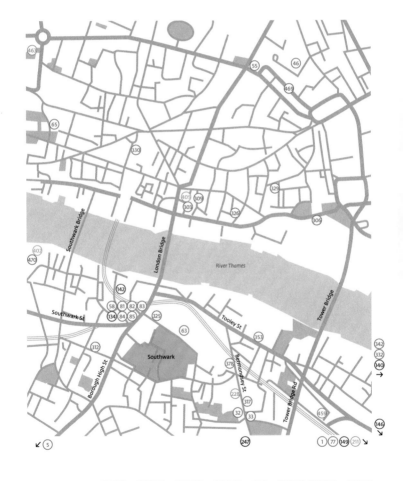

Map 5
SOUTH

King's College
Hospital

Ruskin Park

Brixton Rd

169

3 Coldharbour Ln

307

375

251

Herne Hill Road

Denmark Hill

Milkwood Rd

Brixton Hill

Tulse Hill

Morval Rd

420

Brixton Water Ln

Dulwich Rd

431

212

398

Halfmoon Ln

Brockwell
Park

456

241 ↓

Map 6
SOUTH WEST

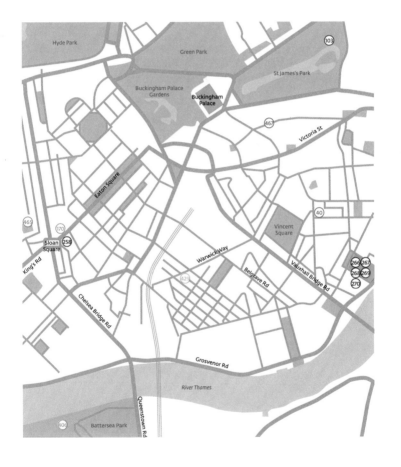

Map 7
WEST

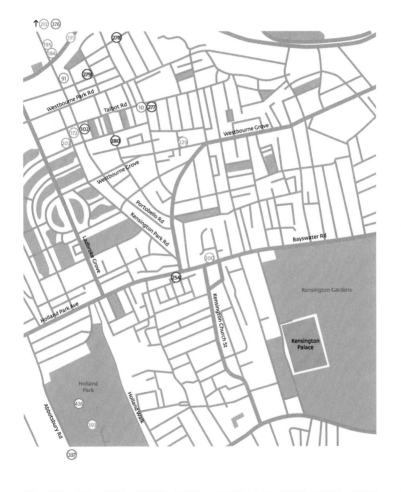

Map 8

MARYLEBONE
and MAYFAIR

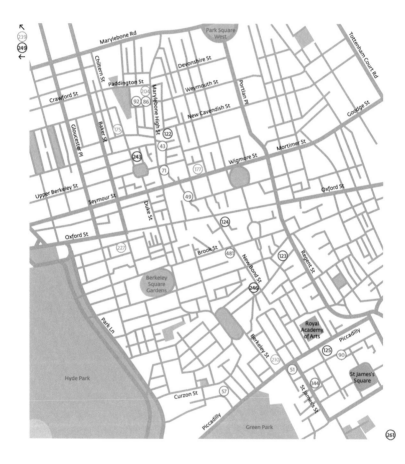

Map 9
HACKNEY

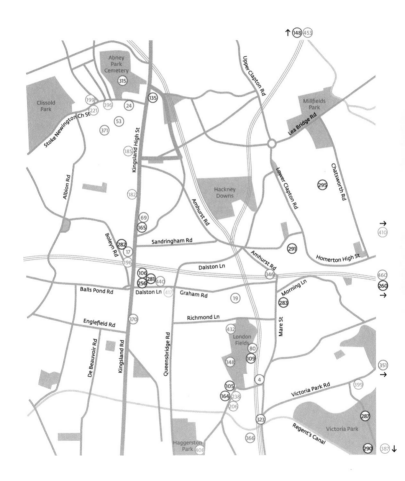

Map 10
NORTH

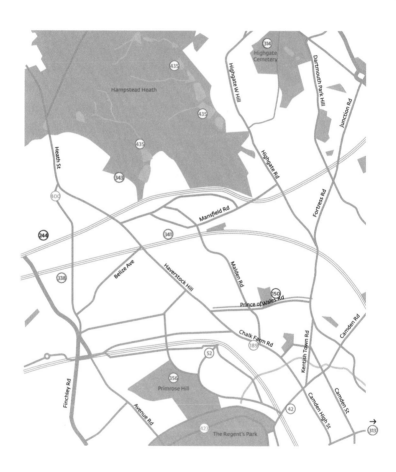

Map 11
ISLINGTON

95 PLACES TO EAT OR BUY GOOD FOOD

The 5 best places for
STREET FOOD

1 MALTBY STREET MARKET
ROPEWALK
41 Maltby St
SE1 3PA
Southbank ④
www.maltby.st

At this lively and atmospheric weekend market vendors have set up their stalls in units beneath railway arches and in the narrow alleyway known as the Ropewalk. Here you will find some of the best producers in town including Hansen and Lydersen, Little Bird Gin, St John's Bakery and Band of Bandits.

2 SOUTHBANK CENTRE MARKET
SOUTHBANK CENTRE
Belvedere Road
SE1 8XX
Southbank ④
www.southbankcentre.co.uk

This street food market is open every Friday to Sunday. It's a great location to eat if you are visiting any of the cultural centres in the South Bank area. The vendors here represent the best in street food cuisine from Britain and around the world. There are often free events and concerts in the Festival Hall in the afternoons.

3 BRIXTON VILLAGE
GRANVILLE ARCADE
Coldharbour Lane
SW9 8PR
South ⑤
www.wearebrixtonvillage. london

Try Franco Manca for pizza, Honest Burgers or Mama Lan's for Beijing street food. There's a nearby outdoor food market and the Market Row arcade has more eating options.

4 NETIL MARKET

13-23 Westgate St
E8 3RL
Hackney ⑨
+44 (0)20 3095 9718
www.eatworkart.com/
netil-market

In the week this is a platform for small creative businesses to sell their clothes, jewellery, ceramics and design products. Saturday is market day, and this is when street food stalls join in, including Bao Bar for Taiwanese steamed buns and Lemlem kitchen for modern African and Eritrean.

5 MERCATO METROPOLITANO

42 Newington Causeway
SE1 6DR
Southbank ④
+44 (0)20 7403 0930
www.mercatometro
politano.co.uk

Housed in a vast former paper factory this covered market is home to an exciting array of street food and artisanal produce stalls, bars and cafes, with a focus on Italian culinary culture. MM is also home to the Backyard Cinema, a community garden and events such as terrarium and gnocchi workshops and vintage fairs.

1 MALTBY STREET

5 *must eat restaurants for*
FOODIES

---

6 **ST JOHN**
26 St John St
EC1M 4AY
+44 (0)20 7251 0848
Clerkenwell ②
*www.stjohngroup.uk.com/
smithfield*

Fergus Henderson has been pioneering his unique style of 'nose to tail' eating since 1994. St John champions traditional and often overlooked elements of British cuisine, with an emphasis on less fashionable cuts of meat. For many visiting chefs a trip here is a priority and a pilgrimage, a place of unpretentious excellence.

7 **BARRAFINA**
26-27 Dean St
W1D 3LL
Soho ①
+44 (0)20 7440 1456
www.barrafina.co.uk

London's best tapas restaurant, and perhaps one of its very best restaurants altogether. Situated in the heart of Soho, you can expect a lively atmosphere here where no reservations are taken, and a queue can be expected unless you arrive at the beginning of service. Any wait is always worth the while though, as once seated at the bar you'll be eating exciting dishes prepared right before you. Two further restaurants, with different menus, have recently opened in the Covent Garden area.

8 MORO

34-36 Exmouth Market
EC1R 4QE
Clerkenwell ②
+44 (0)20 7833 8336
www.moro.co.uk

In the interesting little Exmouth Market area you are spoilt for choice when eating out, but Moro should be your first stop. The food here successfully and inventively marries influences from Moorish Spain and North Africa. If you want a less formal dining experience then try the adjacent Morito tapas bar where the food is just as good.

9 OTTOLENGHI

287 Upper St
N1 2TZ
Islington ⑪
+44 (0)20 7288 1454
*www.ottolenghi.co.uk/
islington*

It is impossible to walk past the window of this deli/restaurant and its inviting display of colourful salads and patisseries. Yotam Ottolenghi's unique style, a blend of influences from his native Israel mixed with flavours and ingredients from across the Mediterranean and Middle East, has found a cult following in London. Dining here is quite informal and good value, but try his Nopi restaurant in Soho for a more refined version.

10 THE LEDBURY

127 Ledbury Road
W11 2AQ
West ⑦
+44 (0)20 7792 9090
www.theledbury.com

Australian chef Brett Graham has created a classic modern British dining experience. Located in a swish part of Notting Hill, the interiors are luxurious and the service is exemplary. The food is memorable, and there is an incredible wine list to match. A must-try for the foodie who's looking for the big budget blow-out experience.

The 5 best places to grab
LUNCH IN SOHO

11 **DUCKSOUP**
41 Dean St
W1D 4PY
Soho ①
+44 (0)20 7287 4599
www.ducksoupsoho.co.uk

The menu of this cosy, narrow little European bistro changes almost daily and the food is simple, ingredient-led and seasonal, full of flavour and often betraying an Italian influence. Wines are all natural and biodynamic, and the by-the-glass menu changes regularly. There's a record player in the corner where you can choose what to play.

12 **PIZZA PILGRIMS**
11 Dean St
W1D 3RP
Soho ①
+44 (0)207 287 8964
www.pizzapilgrims.co.uk

Pizza Pilgrims evolved from a market stall in Berwick Street and specialises in Neapolitan sourdough pizza, using fresh, authentic ingredients, cooked in a stone-baked oven. The green-checked tablecloths suggest an old-school Soho vibe. Sit in the windows or on the street outside to really take in the Soho ambience. The pizzas are delicious and great value. Try the Nutella and salted ricotta pizza ring for dessert.

13 COPITA

27 D'Arblay St
W1F 8EP
Soho ⓘ
+44 (0)20 7287 7797
www.copita.co.uk

Tucked away in a Soho side street, Copita is a bustling tapas bar serving delicious 3-4 bite small plates, such as sherry-braised pig cheeks or jamon Iberico. Lively and informal, the tables are shared or you can sit or stand at the bar. *Copita* means 'small glasses' and there is a great list of wines and sherries, all served by the glass, or try the San Sebastian style gin and tonics.

14 KOYA BAR

50 Frith St
W1D 4SQ
Soho ⓘ
www.koyabar.co.uk

Koya is a super-authentic Japanese udon bar where it quite easy to imagine you're eating out in Tokyo. The interiors are minimalist but warm with plenty of wood on display in this long, narrow space where all the seats are along a bar. Watch the chefs at work on a wealth of udon, ramen and rice dishes, such as *kinoko hiya-atsu* (mushroom and walnut miso).

15 POLPETTO

11 Berwick St
W1F 0PL
Soho ⓘ
+44 (0)20 7439 8627
www.polpetto.co.uk

Hustle past the market stalls and street food vendors on Berwick Street and dive into this Venetian-inspired restaurant for a taste of Italy. Rather small and atmospheric with low lighting and lace-curtained windows, this is the little sister of the successful Polpo restaurants. There are lots of small plates to try, such as veal-cheeks in fennel and bean stew, and the cocktails are good too.

The 5 hippest places to eat in
EAST LONDON

---

16 CAMPANIA AND JONES
23 Ezra St
E2 7RH
East ③
+44 (0)20 7613 0015
www.campania
andjones.com

Housed in a ramshackle former dairy building, and located on a cobbled side street off Columbia Road, this cafe-style Italian restaurant enjoys a charming and atmospheric setting. The short daily menus feature homemade pastas – tortelli, pappardelle, gnudi – and incredibly tasty dishes of authentic, domestic Italian cooking.

17 VOODOO RAY'S
95 Kingsland High St
E8 2PB
Hackney ⑨
+44 (0)20 7249 7865
www.voodoorays.com

Named after A Guy Called Gerald's UK acid house anthem, Voodoo Ray's is the place to come if you're on a night out in Dalston and its many bars and clubs. 22" NY-style pizzas are served by the slice, with dance music-referencing names such as the Hot Mix 5 and Giorgio Moroder. Open until 3 am, frozen margaritas are mixed in a slush machine and the Full Moon Slice only comes out after midnight. Fun.

18 THE MARKSMAN

254 Hackney Road
E2 7SJ
Hackney ③
+44 (0)20 7739 7393
*www.marksman
publichouse.com*

This revamped Victorian boozer in Hackney manages to retain its old-school charm despite the makeover. The food here is seriously good and worth a trip, but The Marksman still functions as a proper drinking pub, attracting a hip younger crowd as well as the older locals. Try the braised beef and barley bun with horseradish.

19 PIDGIN

52 Wilton Way
E8 1BS
Hackney ⑨
+44 (0)20 7254 8311
www.pidginlondon.com

Located on a quiet Hackney backstreet, Pidgin is the next project from James Ramsden and Sam Herlihy after the success of their Secret Larder supper club. Almost as convivial, this space is intimate with minimal décor other than twigs and branches on the walls. The cooking is vibrant modern British with an Asian twist.

20 TYPING ROOM
AT: TOWN HALL HOTEL

Patriot Square
E2 9NF
East ③
+44 (0)20 7871 0461
www.typingroom.com

Perhaps a little too upmarket to be truly hipsterish, this is certainly one of East London's hottest restaurants. Located in the former secretarial offices of the imposing old Bethnal green town hall building, Typing Room serves intricately constructed modernist dishes with a Nordic influence. There are lots of foraged ingredients, petals and plenty of smoking and curing going on here.

The 5 best
VEGETARIAN
restaurants

---

21 THE GALLERY CAFE

St. Margaret's House
Settlement
21 Old Ford Road
E2 9PL
East ③
+44 (0)20 8980 2092
www.stmargaretshouse.
org.uk/thegallerycafe

This vegetarian cafe is located in a community charity building in Bethnal Green. The space doubles as an art gallery and events venue. The Gallery Cafe is a real cultural and community hub with live music, comedy and a book club among the other activities that happen here. The menu is fairly basic but good value, and there's a lovely outdoor space in the summer.

22 MILDREDS

45 Lexington St
WF1 9AN
Soho ①
+44 (0)20 7494 1634
www.mildreds.co.uk

Mildreds is a popular Soho institution that was founded in the 1980s. They don't take reservations, so at busy times you may have to wait. In which case you could try one of their excellent cocktails at the bar. There's an intimate and cosy atmosphere here, and the food will leave you with a warm feeling too, much of it influenced by the Middle East and Asia.

23 WILD FOOD CAFE

14 Neal's Yard
WC2H 9DP
Covent Garden ①
+44 (0)20 7419 2014
www.wildfoodcafe.com

In a secret courtyard in Covent Garden, where alternative enterprises have thrived since the 1970s, the Wild Food Cafe is located on the first floor of an old warehouse building. After you've checked out Neil's Yard Remedies and the yoga and massage places, head up the stairs and enjoy the raw-centric cooking and superfoods on offer. There's a communal vibe at the shared wooden tables.

24 RASA N16

55 Stoke Newington
Church St
N16 0AR
Hackney ⑨
+44 (0)20 7249 0344
www.rasarestaurants.com

This East London veggie curry house specialises in authentic Keralan cuisine from spice-rich Southern India. Small and cosy, you can't miss the bright pink paintwork of the frontage on the street. The food is fresh and fragrant, and very good value. In Sanskrit the word rasa implies taste, pleasure and affection. You won't be disappointed.

25 THE GATE

51 Queen Caroline St
Hammersmith
W6 9QL
West ⑦
+44 (0)20 8748 6932
thegaterestaurants.com

The Gate has had a reputation since 1989 for being one of London's few fine dining vegetarian places. Once you have navigated the hidden entrance, go upstairs to the elegant and airy dining room. The food here is a mix of Mediterranean and Asian influences, beautifully presented, with earthy, gusty flavours. A sister venue in Islington opened recently.

The 5 best
ASIAN
restaurants

---

26   BAO

53 Lexington St
W1F 9AS
Soho ①
www.baolondon.com

This Taiwanese street food-inspired joint has quickly earned a cult following. The speciality is the *bao*, a steamed bun, served with a variety of delicious fillings such as braised pork and peanut powder. All dishes are *xiao chi* (small eats) and incredibly tasty, fresh and innovative. A must try, even if you have to queue across the street to get in.

27   ESARN KHEAW

314 Uxbridge Road
W12 7LJ
West ⑦
+44 (0)20 8743 8930
www.esarnkheaw.com

This family-run locals' favourite in Shepherd's Bush is known for its super authentic North Eastern Thai cuisine. The occasionally eccentric service and slightly tired traditional décor only add to the charm. The flavours here are unusual, fresh and deeply satisfying.

28   SUSHINO EN

2 White Church Lane
E1 7QR
East ③
+44 (0)20 3645 6734
www.sushinoen.com

This stylish and modern Japanese restaurant is a great find. The sushi is technically spot-on, a mixture of classic and modern fusion options. The sashimi and noodle, rice and grilled dishes are also of high quality. The basement houses a karaoke room.

29 JOY KING LAU

3 Leicester St
WC2H 7BL
Soho ①
+44 (0)20 7437 1132
www.joykinglau.com

With Joy King Lau you're in reliably good hands in this cosy yet unassuming-looking room on the third floor. The speciality here is the freshly-made dim sum, steamed or fried, which are only served before 5 pm. The rest of the menu is on-point too though, and good value. If you've room left then try the deep fried custard bun for dessert.

30 SHILPA

206 King St
W6 0RA
West ⑦
+44 (0)20 8741 3127
www.shilparestaurant.co.uk

This Indian in Hammersmith is a neighbourhood favourite that's worth making a trip for. Family-run and incredibly friendly, the Keralan food here is authentic yet modern. Freshly-cooked dishes such as Avial, Sea Bass Thengapal Roast and Aattirachi Varattigathu (spiced lamb) reveal a mastery of spicing with their wonderful flavours.

26 BAO

The 5 best restaurants for
INTERNATIONAL CUISINE

---

31 **TRULLO**

300-302 St Paul's Road
N1 2LH
Islington ⑪
+44 (0)20 7226 2733
www.trullorestaurant.com

Named after the traditional conical stone huts found in Puglia, the food here is similarly elegant, rustic and unpretentious. The menu is constantly changing with the seasons, but a few things always remain: the warm ambiance, the superb freshly-made pasta and the famous dish of pappardelle with beef shin ragu.

32 **JOSÉ TAPAS BAR**

104 Bermondsey St
SE1 3UB
Southbank ④
+44 (0)20 7403 4902
*www.josepizarro.com/
jose-tapas-bar*

Seating is limited and, as this can be a lively and popular spot, there's a good chance you'll have to stand, just as you would in Spain. The classic tapas served here are perfectly created and the wine list is excellent to match.

33 **CASSE-CROÛTE**

109 Bermondsey St
SE1 3XB
Southbank ④
+44 (0)20 7407 2140
www.cassecroute.co.uk

Intimate, rustic and charming, no cliché seems to have been avoided in decking this place out in true Gallic style. The cooking is hearty and full of flavour and there are daily-changing specials. Convivial.

34 **BRASSERIE ZEDEL**

20 Sherwood St
W1F 7ED
Soho ①
+44 (0)20 7734 4888
www.brasseriezedel.com

Zedel's is a brasserie in the grand European style. At street level it appears only to be a small cafe, but once you have descended the stairs the opulence and scale of this operation will amaze. Apart from the cocktail bar and cabaret spot there is a huge high-ceilinged dining hall in the Art Deco/Beaux Arts style. They serve up classic fare such as *steak haché* and duck confit, all at incredibly reasonable prices.

35 **THE RED SEA**

382 Uxbridge Road
W12 7LL
West ⑦
+44 (0)20 8749 6888

This unusual restaurant specialises in cuisine from around the Horn of Africa: Ethiopia, Eritrea, Somalia and Yemen. The setting is somewhat ramshackle but the food is interesting. That you can take your own alcohol makes this place even better value.

32 JOSÉ TAPAS BAR

The 5 best
GREASY SPOON CAFES

---

36 E PELLICCI

332 Bethnal Green Road
E2 0AG
East ③
+44 (0)20 7739 4873

Pellici's is an East End institution. This working man's cafe has been in the same Italian family since opening in 1900. The wonderful Art Deco interior, with its formica tables and marquetry, dates from 1946 and is listed by English Heritage. Yet this is no relic, but rather a very much alive and vibrant place, full of East End banter. The food here is classic fry-up fare with the addition of Italian specials and some good puddings.

37 TERRY'S

158 Great Suffolk St
SE1 1PE
Southbank ④
+44 (0)20 7407 9358
www.terryscafe.co.uk

Terry's has been a South London locals' favourite since 1982, although it is now run by his son Austin. This friendly spot has a traditional look, and will serve up the perfect all-day English breakfast, as well as menu items such as bubble and squeak and toad-in-the-hole.

38 MARIE'S CAFE

90 Lower Marsh
SE1 7AB
Southbank ④
+44 (0)20 7928 1050

Marie's offers a unique proposition: by day it is the classic greasy spoon cafe, in the evening it turns into a super-value Thai restaurant. Located behind Waterloo Station, the appearance from the outside is unremarkable and the interior is equally unassuming, but the welcome is warm and the food keeps the regulars returning.

39 ANDREW'S RESTAURANT

160 Grays Inn Road
WC1X 8ED
Clerkenwell ②
+44 (0)20 7837 1630

Andrew's is a superior traditional workers' cafe that attracts a dedicated and mixed crowd of diners. The cheery interior features formica tables, lino flooring and 'outsider art' paintings of black cabs and red buses on the city streets. A vast chalkboard details the multiple and varied cooked breakfast and lunchtime menu options. The tea is good and strong and the grub not too greasy.

40 REGENCY CAFE

17-19 Regency St
SW1P 4BY
South West ⑥
+44 (0)20 7821 6596

Situated in a quiet Pimlico street this cafe has the appearance of the archetypal English fry up place, retaining its original tiling and atmosphere. It has often featured as a location in period cinema and drama. There's a woman who booms out the orders as they're ready, and the food is good and reliable, with dishes such as steak pie with chips and gravy. Twin with a trip to nearby Tate Britain.

The 5 best places for
FISH AND CHIPS

---

41 POPPIE'S
6-8 Hanbury St
E1 6QR
East ③
+44 (0)20 7247 0892
*www.poppiesfishandchips.
co.uk*

Poppie's sports a kitsch 'modern retro' 1950s look complete with jukebox and fake newsprint to serve up in. However, the food is of a very high standard, with fish sourced sustainably from Billingsgate Market. Prices here are not quite as nostalgic as the vintage feel.

42 HOOK CAMDEN TOWN
63-65 Parkway
NW1 7PP
North ⑩
+44 (0)20 3808 5112
www.hookrestaurants.com

Hook offers clever, innovative twists on the classic F&C template. The sustainably sourced fish is perfectly cooked with crispy batters and is served in a bright and contemporary setting with communal tables. Try Cajun spiced hake, Jamaican jerk panko or one of the freshly-caught daily specials, finished off with an exciting array of customised condiments.

43 THE GOLDEN HIND

73 Marylebone Lane
W1U 2PN
Marylebone ⑧
+44 (0)20 7486 3644

Tucked away on a cobbled side street in Marylebone, this venerable operation has been in business since 1914. The standard here is very high indeed, and it brings in a loyal and mixed crowd to the comfortable dining room. The Hind is great value, and you can bring in your own alcohol too. The real thing.

44 GOLDEN UNION

38 Poland St
W1F 7LY
Soho ①
+44 (0)20 7434 1933
www.goldenunion.co.uk

Golden Union is a modern venture in Soho with the knowingly retro feel of an authentic chips shop. The fish and chips here are reliably good. They use a special mix of delicate oils and a light beer batter which delivers a delicious, crisp and golden product.

45 THE FRYER'S DELIGHT

19 Theobalds Road
WC1X 8SL
Clerkenwell ②
+44 (0)20 7405 4114

This Holborn chippy is very much from the old school, dating back to 1962 and with original furnishing and fixtures in the interior. They use beef dripping in their oil, which, though not ideal for vegetarians, does impart a wonderful rich flavour to anything coming out of the fryer.

The 5 best places for
MEAT EATERS

---

46 **PITT CUE CO.**

1 Devonshire Square
EC2M 4YP
City ④
+44 (0)20 7324 7770
www.pittcue.co.uk

Pitt Cue has quickly evolved from its humble street food origins, recently relocating to larger premises. The expanded menu puts the custom-built wood-burning grill to good use with dishes such as Mangalitza chop and grilled lamb heart. They now take reservations and there's the added attraction of an in-house brewery.

47 **HAWKSMOOR**

157A Commercial St
E1 6BJ
East ③
+44 (0)20 7426 4850
www.thehawksmoor.com/
locations/spitalfields

Named after Nicholas Hawksmoor's nearby Christ Church, the menu here is almost as imposing and occult. This place is all about meat, and in particular beef. Whether you have the Chateaubriand, T-bone, porterhouse, rib or the matured steaks (served by the 100 gram) the quality will be the very highest. The triple-cooked chips won't disappoint either, and the cocktails and breakfasts here are certainly worth a visit in their own right.

48 SMOKING GOAT

7 Denmark St
WC2H 8LZ
Covent Garden ①
www.smokinggoatsoho.com

Nestled amongst the fading glories of London's Tin Pan Alley, this atmospheric dive-bar no-reservation restaurant specialises in wood-smoked Thai BBQ, rare breed meats and offal. Rich and smoky cuts cosy up to spicy and fragrant Thai flavours, making for a lip-smacking combination. Try the Chiang Mai BBQ Pork Belly.

49 MEATLIQUOR

74 Welbeck St
W1G 0BA
Marylebone ⑧
+44 (0)20 7224 4239
www.meatliquor.com

MEATliquor offers a simple-yet-winning concept. Delicious US-style chicken, burgers and 'dogs' are served alongside a huge and dangerous cocktail list. The décor here is graffiti-splattered, the lighting is on the dark side of low, and the noise of the enthusiastic diners and background music can be very loud. MEATmission is a sister branch housed in an old church in Hoxton.

50 FLAT IRON

17 Beak St
W1F 9RW
Soho ①
www.flatironsteak.co.uk

Yes, this is another US-style meat joint that doesn't take reservations, so it's perfectly on-trend. Flat Iron doesn't offer much in the way of a menu, but what it does it does very well. The signature steaks, lean and marbled, come scorched on the outside and pink in the middle. The queueing system is at least fairly enlightened – they send a text to your phone when they're ready, allowing you to wait in a nearby pub or bar until the time to chow down arrives.

5 places for a
FABULOUS BREAKFAST

---

51 **THE WOLSELEY**

160 Piccadilly
W1J 9EB
Mayfair ⑧
+44 (0)20 7499 6996
www.thewolseley.com

The dining room at The Wolseley is a grand Art Deco space that was originally used as a luxury car showroom, but now houses this opulent Viennese brasserie. There is a real sense of occasion here, and the breakfasts more than live up to it. Eggs Arnold Bennett, devilled lamb kidneys, haggis with duck eggs or perfect eggs benedict: there are many rich options if you are feeling decadent. The Viennoiserie are excellent, and coffee is served in a silver pot.

52 **GREENBERRY CAFE**

101 Regent's Park Road
NW1 8UR
North ⑩
+44 (0)20 7483 3765
wwwgreenberrycafe.co.uk

Well-situated amongst the independent shops in pretty Primrose Hill, the Greenberry Cafe is a popular and attractive spot. The breakfast (and at the weekend, brunch) menu is served until 3 pm. There's an emphasis on healthy options such as quinoa porridge with chopped dates. Or try the waffles with maple-glazed bacon, poached eggs and avocado.

53 **ESTERS**
55 Kynaston Road
N16 0EB
Hackney ⑨
+44 (0)20 7254 0253
www.estersn16.com

Esters cafe is a neighbourhood favourite in Stoke Newington with a laid-back and cheery atmosphere. It serves up the best breakfasts in the area, and brunch at the weekend. St John bakery supplies bread and cakes and excellent coffee comes from Has Bean and guest roasters. The menu here is ever-changing and often surprising.

54 **THE HABIT**
AT SOUTH LONDON GALLERY
67 Peckham Road
SE5 8UH
South ⑤
+44 (0)20 7252 7649
www.thehabitlondon.co.uk

The Habit is located in a Victorian terrace building adjacent to Peckham's impressive South London Gallery. There's a good atmosphere and an artsy vibe, with breakfasts and weekend brunches here being justifiably popular. There are many fresh juices and interesting healthy options, with brunch being served from 8.30 am until 4 pm every day.

55 **DUCK & WAFFLE**
HERON TOWER
110 Bishopsgate
EC2N 4AY
City ④
+44 (0)20 3640 7310
www.duckandwaffle.com

With its floor-to-ceiling windows and amazing 40th floor views across the city, this is the place to come for a special breakfast to remember. The signature dish here is two fluffy Belgian waffles served with duck confit, fried duck eggs and maple syrup. The rest of the menu doesn't disappoint either (avoid the 'Full Elvis').

The 5 best restaurants for a
ROMANTIC MEAL

56 J SHEEKEY

28-35 St Martin's Court
WC2N 4AL
Covent Garden ①
+44 (0)20 7240 2565
www.j-sheekey.co.uk

Sheekey's is a West End institution, and has been serving quality seafood since it opened in 1896. It exudes an old-fashioned glamour, with photos of film and theatre stars adorning the walls, secluded tables and a very high level of service. The fish pie here is famous, comforting yet seductive at the same time, or you could try more refined dishes such as Dover sole with béarnaise. For a less formal date try their equally stylish Oyster Bar next door.

57 KITTY FISHER'S

10 Shepherd Market
W1J 7QF
Mayfair ⑧
+44 (0)20 3302 1661
www.kittyfishers.com

Located in Mayfair's historic Shepherd Market, this is an intimate and dimly lit place with a real old-world charm. Kitty Fisher herself was an infamous 18th-century courtesan who operated in the market's once less than salubrious warren of streets. The food here is modern British with a Spanish touch, much of it cooked on a smoky wooden grill. Try the anchovy, mint and parsley lamb cutlets.

58 WRIGHT BROTHERS OYSTER AND PORTER HOUSE

11 Stoney St
SE1 9AD
Southbank ④
+44 (0)20 7403 9554
www.thewrightbrothers.
co.uk

If you're susceptible to the aphrodisiac powers of the oyster then this lively bar restaurant next to Borough Market could be a good venue for a fun date. Here you can try oysters from Britain, Ireland, France and from further afield, and compare their different tastes and textures. There are plenty of other crustacean and seafood options available, and a fine range of sparkling and white wines in addition to the porter ales on offer.

59 BERNERS TAVERN

10 Berners St
W1T 3LF
Soho ①
+44 (0)20 7908 7979
www.bernerstavern.com

The Berners Tavern has one of the most dazzling dining rooms in London, a perfect place for an impressive romantic date. Large and low lit, with ornate stuccoed high-ceilings, a luminous backlit gold bar and paintings of different styles and sizes covering nearly every inch of the walls, its glamour takes the breath away. The modern British food manages to live up to its surroundings somehow.

60 ANDREW EDMUNDS

46 Lexington St
W1F 0LP
Soho ①
+44 (0)20 7437 5708
www.andrewedmunds.com

Exuding a cosy old-school charm, this intimate candlelit restaurant is located in a rather cramped 18th-century town house, adjacent to a dimly lit gallery of the same name selling antique prints and satirical drawings. The food is a pleasing mix of comforting British and European bistro classics; the wine list of exceptional value.

5 restaurants with a
GREAT VIEW

61 **SKYLON**
Royal Festival Hall
Belvedere Road
SE1 8XX
Southbank ④
+44 (0)20 7654 7800
*www.skylon-restaurant.
co.uk*

The Skylon was a temporary space-age structure built for the Festival of Britain that symbolised post-war optimism. It stood next to the Royal Festival Hall, where this restaurant, which serves modern European cuisine in a smart setting, is now situated on an upper floor overlooking the river Thames. In addition to the concerts and cultural events that take place here, it is another good reason to visit.

62 **LEVEL 6 RESTAURANT**
AT TATE MODERN
Bankside
E1 9TG
Southbank ④
+44 (0)20 7887 8888
*www.tate.org.uk/visit/
tate-modern/eat-drink-and-
shop/level-6-restaurant*

After spending a few hours taking in the art collections, special exhibitions and buildings at Tate Modern you'll very likely need a sit down, and probably some food as well. This restaurant is located on an upper floor of the original power station building, has full length windows and enjoys wonderful, ever-changing views across the river towards St Paul's cathedral and the city beyond. It's not especially cheap, but the revenues support the work of the gallery.

63 HUTONG
LEVEL 33 THE SHARD

31 St Thomas Street
SE1 9RY
Southbank ④
+44 (0)20 3011 1257
www.hutong.co.uk

Occupying the 33rd floor of the enormous yet somehow elegant Shard building, this upmarket restaurant serves Sichuan and North Chinese cuisine. The panoramic views here are really special indeed, even from the toilets that are precipitously positioned right up against the glass. The food is high quality and authentic.

64 NATIONAL PORTRAIT GALLERY RESTAURANT

National Portrait Gallery
St Martin's Place
WC2H 0HE
Covent Garden ②
+44 (0)20 7312 2490
www.npg.org.uk/visit/shop-eat-drink.php

The restaurant at the Portrait Gallery is right at the top of the building, and it offers tremendous views of the central London skyline. The view extends across Trafalgar Square, taking in Nelson's Column, Whitehall, Big Ben, the Houses of Parliament and as far as the London Eye on the South Bank. It's open for breakfast, lunch and afternoon tea as well as some evenings, serving modern British fare.

65 BARBECOA

20 New Change Passage
EC4M 9AG
City ④
+44 (0)20 3005 8555
www.barbecoa.com

The imposing view here is dominated by the eastern aspect of the magnificent St Paul's Cathedral, designed by Christopher Wren in 1675. Barbecoa serves a variety of high quality meat dishes, which are cooked using various techniques including Texas pit smoker, Argentine grill, Japanese robata grill, tandoor and wood-fired oven. There's an in-house butchery and dry-aging store.

The 5 tastiest
CHEAP EATS

---

66 **SÔNG QUÊ CAFE**
   134 Kingsland Road
   E2 8DY
   East ③
   +44 (0)20 7613 3222

This stretch of Kingsland Road is renowned for its cluster of Vietnamese restaurants. Sông Quê is the pick for its lively atmosphere. There are more than 20 variations of pho noodle soup dishes. Queues are likely and service can be perfunctory but it's more than worth it.

67 **ABU ZAAD**
   29 Uxbridge Road
   W12 8LH
   West ⑦
   +44 (0)20 8749 5107
   www.abuzaad.co.uk

This neighbourhood favourite serves 'Damascene' dishes from Syria. Mixed grills, kebabs and koftes are also recommended, along with the interesting drink options such as *ayran* (a salty yoghurt drink), fresh lemonades, juices and mint tea.

68 **TAYYABS**
   83-89 Fieldgate St
   E1 1JU
   East ③
   +44 (0)20 7247 6400
   www.tayyabs.co.uk

This legendary Punjabi restaurant has been an institution since 1972. It can get very busy here in the evenings, the crowds arriving to sample the incredibly good value food that is rich, aromatic and satisfying in flavour. Tasty lamb chops are served smoking on a skillet and the dry curries are a must-try too.

69 MANGAL 1

10 Arcola St, off Stoke
Newington Road
E8 2DJ
Hackney ⑨
+44 (0)20 7275 8981
www.mangal1.com

This Turkish place is hidden away on a side street just off Kingsland Road in Dalston, and serves delicious *ocakbasi*, food cooked on an open-coal barbecue. The smoking grill is right by the entrance and you may have to queue to get past it. A new branch called Mangal 1.1 has now opened in Shoreditch.

70 YALLA YALLA

1 Green's Court
W1F 0HA
Soho ①
+44 (0)20 7287 7663
www.yalla-yalla.co.uk

This tiny modern Lebanese is found down a dingy alley in Soho. It's a smart and intimate setting from where they serve Beirut street food to a small number of tables or to take away. Try the delicious Sawda Djej, sautéed chicken livers with garlic and pomegranate molasses, or the Kibbhe Lahme. There is a larger twin branch in Fitzrovia.

69 MANGAL 1

The 5 best specialist
FOOD *and* DRINK
SHOPS

71 **PAUL ROTHE & SON**
35 Marylebone Lane
W1U 2NN
Marylebone ⑧
+44 (0)20 7935 6783
www.paulrotheandson
delicatessen.co.uk

This cafe, sandwich shop, delicatessen and grocer's is a wonderful piece of old-fashioned England. It has been in the same family since 1900 and the charming interior appears not to have been updated since at least the 60s. The speciality here is jarred comestibles, especially jams and preserves, but also relishes, pickles and condiments, as well as biscuits.

72 **THE SAMPLER**
266 Upper St
N1 2UQ
Islington ⑪
+44 (0)20 7226 9500
www.thesampler.co.uk

This wine merchant stocks over 1500 carefully chosen and unusual wines from small producers around the world, specialising in mature vintages. At any one time there are up to 80 wines available to sample and taste, at a small charge but with no pressure to buy.

73 GERRY'S WINES AND SPIRITS

74 Old Compton St
W1D 4UW
Soho ①
+44 (0)20 7734 2053
gerrys.uk.com

Gerry's is a Soho stalwart specialising in rare and exotic spirits. It's a small but very crowded store that packs in a huge range of bottles from all over the world with well over 100 varieties each of tequila, vodka, gin, whisky and rum as well as absinthes, piscos, vermouths and much more. Every bottle has it's own distinctive hand-written description and recommendation.

74 PLANET ORGANIC

22 Torrington Place
WC1E 7HJ
Bloomsbury ②
+44 (0)20 7436 1929
www.planetorganic.com

Specialising in organic, vegetarian and vegan produce and ethical products this large store has an incredibly wide range on offer. There is also a cafe and delicatessen with excellent juices, wraps, salads and hot foods that are available to take away. There are also branches in Islingston, Notting Hill and the City.

75 HOXTON STREET MONSTER SUPPLIES

159 Hoxton St
N1 6PJ
Shoreditch
East ③
www.monstersupplies.org

A very curious enterprise indeed, this sweet shop caters to monsters, vampires and werewolves as well as the occasional human being, purveying 'bespoke and everyday items for the living, dead and undead.' It's a delightful emporium selling products such as cubed earwax, fang floss, banshee balls and obscure remedies. Profits are diverted to the Ministry of Stories - a children's charity promoting creative writing.

The 5 best places for
BAKERY and CAKES

76 **FABRIQUE**
   8 Earlham St
   WC2H 9RY
   Covent Garden ①
   +44 (0)20 7240 1392
   www.fabrique.co.uk

Founded in Stockholm, this bakery and cafe has recently brought its artisanal sourdough expertise to London. Housed in an on-trend retro-industrial chic interior, they produce high quality breads and Swedish buns. The sticky, aromatic cardamom buns are a must-try, although the cinnamon and saffron ones are almost as good. If you fancy a fika (coffee break) they serve that too.

77 **ST JOHN**
   Ropewalk
   SE1 2HQ
   Southbank ④
   +44 (0)20 7553 9844
   *www.stjohngroup.uk.com/
   maltby_street*

The actual bakery is just behind on Druid Street (open only weekends), but come to this cafe instead for a chance to sit down and enjoy the produce. As well as the first-rate bread they sell the imperiously rich and sticky Eccles cakes and the generously filled, indulgent custard and chocolate doughnuts for which St John is renowned. They also serve a small repertoire from the St John restaurant canon and the best bacon sarnie in town..

78 MAISON BERTAUX

28 Greek St
W1D 5DQ
Soho ①
+44 (0)20 7437 6007
www.maisonbertaux.com

This 19th-century French patisserie has been a Soho stronghold since 1871. It is a rather quaint and old-fashioned cafe serving a rich array of cakes, bakeries and patisseries such as raspberry éclair and excellent croissants. Whether you sit outside on the street, in the cafe or upstairs you will be able to enjoy the ever-changing Soho life unfold before you.

79 BRICK LANE BEIGEL BAKE

159 Brick Lane
E1 6SB
East ③
+44 (0)20 7729 0616

Open 24 hours a day, this atmospheric New York-style beigel bakery has been in business since 1977. It bakes the perfect beigel: warm and fresh, soft and chewy inside and lightly crunchy on the outside. The hot salt-beef, pickle and mustard beigel is a must-try here. It always seems to be busy, and is very popular with East London's late-night revellers.

80 E5 BAKEHOUSE

Arch 395
Mentmore Terrace
E8 3PH
Hackney ⑨
+44 (0)20 8986 9600
www.e5bakehouse.com

This artisanal bakery is housed under a railway arch in London Fields. The speciality here is organic sourdough, whether it comes in the form of a seeded rye, raisin and walnut, Hackney wild, or spelt loaf (to name only a few of the varieties on offer). They also produce cakes and pastries and run a lovely cafe. There's a good chance you'll be sufficiently impressed to want to enrol in one of their baking lessons.

The 5 best stalls at
BOROUGH MARKET

Borough Market
8 Southwark St
SE1 1TL
Southbank ④

81 **KAPPACASEIN**
Thursday – Saturday
www.kappacasein.com

Originally a one-man operation it has now expanded into a small Raclette factory due to its popularity. Raclette is a Swiss cheese dish served with small waxy potatoes and pickles. They now sell amazing cheese toasties as well, using three cheeses, onions and sourdough bread. Both snacks are perfectly produced and ready to eat on the spot.

82 **MRS KING'S PORK PIES**
Wednesday – Saturday
www.mrskingsporkpies.
co.uk

This stall is one of the more humble looking and only sells a few products, but they are all of the highest order. The Melton Mowbray company has produced hand-made award-winning pork pies since 1853. Mouth-watering pastry, delicately flavoured jelly and succulent meat result in the delicious savoury pies on offer here. Try the hot sausage rolls.

83   RICHARD HAWARD'S OYSTERS

Tuesday – Saturday
www.richardhawards
oysters.co.uk

The Haward family of oystermen are in their eighth generation of business, which dates back to the 1700s. They farm the oyster beds of Mersea Island in Essex, and produce some of the finest oysters available. Here they are incredibly fresh, best enjoyed shucked on the spot with a dash of lemon and tabasco.

84   SPICE MOUNTAIN

Monday – Saturday
www.spicemountain.co.uk

This independent company specialises in spices, seasonings and dried herbs. The depth and variety of their product range is huge, with spices available from Ethiopia, Japan, Thailand, Mexico, India and more. They offer a number of unique spice blends such as Moroccan Fish Tagine or Lebanese 7 Spice.

85   CHEGWORTH VALLEY

Monday – Saturday
www.chegworthvalley.com

The Chegworth stall is among the most attractive at Borough, selling a colourful and beautifully arranged array of organic farm products, fruit, vegetables and salads, all from the family-run farm in Kent. They have a range of award-winning fruit juices including different apple varieties and rhubarb and beetroot. They've won the Slow Food London 'Best Greengrocer' award twice in a row.

The 5 best shops for
BRITISH PRODUCE

86 THE GINGER PIG
8-10 Moxon St
W1U 4EW
Marylebone ⑧
+44 (0)20 7935 7788
www.thegingerpig.co.uk

The quality of the meat here is first class, be it any cut of beef, pork, lamb or poultry. Most of it is sourced directly from their own farm in the North Yorkshire moors. Their own pastries, pies and epic sausage rolls are of the same standard. Butchery classes are also available.

87 A. GOLD
42 Brushfield St
E1 6AG
East ③
+44 (0)20 7247 2487
www.agoldshop.com

Located next to Spitalfields Market this old-fashioned looking shop sells 'traditional foods of Britain.' Aiming to be 'a village shop in the City,' they sell quintessentially British products such as Henderson's relish and Campbell's Tea.

88 STEVE HATT
88-90 Essex Road
N1 8LU
Islington ⑪
+44 (0)20 7226 3963

Steve is the fourth generation of fishmonger in his family, and their shop has been on this Islington street since 1895. The fish is almost all sourced from UK waters and is good value despite its high quality and freshness. Steve and his staff are knowledgeable and enthusiastic.

89 THE GROCERY

54-56 Kingsland Road
E2 8DP
East ③
+44 (0)20 7729 6855
www.thegroceryshop.co.uk

This attractive grocery store, with vaulted brick ceilings, is located in the heart of Shoreditch and opens late every day. They specialise in organic, fair trade and locally-sourced products. As well as the fruit and vegetables and general groceries there's a deli counter and a cafe at the back of the shop.

90 PAXTON & WHITFIELD

93 Jermyn St
SW1Y 6JE
Mayfair ⑧
+44 (0)20 7930 0259
www.paxtonand
whitfield.co.uk

"A gentleman only buys his cheese from Paxton and Whitfield." So said Winston Churchill, and little has changed in that respect since this cheesemonger was founded in 1797. British cheeses of every stripe are stocked here; Stichelton, Lincolnshire Poacher, Cheddar, Red Leicester and of course Stilton. Every kind of cheese accessory is also available as well as European cheese varieties.

90 PAXTON & WHITFIELD

5 essential

INTERNATIONAL
FOOD STORES

---

91 **R. GARCIA & SONS**

248-250 Portobello Road
W11 1LL
West ⑦
+44 (0)20 7221 6119
www.rgarciaandsons.com

This family-owned Spanish supermarket has been a neighbourhood favourite since 1957. They offer a huge selection of Spanish imported goods such as paella rice, legumes, preserves, spices, and olive oil. There's a good deli section and their Cafe Garcia is next door.

92 **LA FROMAGERIE**

2-6 Moxon St
W1U 4EW
Marylebone ⑧
+44 (0)20 7935 0341
www.lafromagerie.co.uk

This Marylebone grocer offers a high-end range of imported goods and fresh products from France, Italy and the UK. The speciality here is cheese, of course, and there's a walk-in temperature-controlled room with an amazing selection. If you can find a seat, there's an excellent cafe.

93 **PERSEPOLIS**

28-30 Peckham High St
SE15 5DT
South ⑤
+44 (0)20 7639 8007
www.foratasteofpersia.co.uk

This unusual shop offers a 'taste of Persia in Peckham', as well as goods from the Middle East and Levantine countries. There's a charming, arty atmosphere and the shop also sells handicrafts, musical instruments, shishas and coffee makers. There's also a small cafe area.

94 LINA STORES

18 Brewer St
W1F 0SH
Soho ①
+44 (0)20 7437 6482
www.linastores.co.uk

This beautiful store, recently refurbished, has been selling traditional Italian groceries in Soho since 1944. It's been run by the same Genovese family all that time. They sell all kinds of imported Italian brands and products and there's an impressive deli and antipasti selection. In autumn it's a good place to find the best porcini and truffles.

95 RICE WINE

82 Brewer St
W1F 9UA
Soho ①
+44 (0)20 7439 3705
www.ricewine.f2s.com

This small supermarket in Soho supplies an excellent range of good value foods from Japan and the Far East. The interior is rather basic but it's the place to come for sushi rice, wasabi, seaweed, sake, noodles, ramen, colourfully-packaged sweets or rice wine.

94 LINA STORES

SKETCH

70 PLACES
FOR A DRINK

---

5 coffee shops for a serious
CAFFEINE FIX

---

96 KAFFEINE

66 Great Titchfield St
W1W 7QJ
Soho ⓘ
+44 (0)20 7580 6755
www.kaffeine.co.uk

This stylish Australian-style espresso spot in Fitzrovia, just near Oxford Circus, serves fantastic coffee from a Synesso Cyncra machine. The cakes, pastries and changing breakfast and lunch menus are excellent too, and their beans are available for retail.

97 ALGERIAN COFFEE STORES

52 Old Compton St
W1D 4PB
Soho ⓘ
+44 (0)20 7437 2480
www.algcoffee.co.uk

A fixture in Soho since 1887 the Algerian Coffee Store sells more than 80 varieties of coffee beans from around the world. The atmospheric store is packed full of coffee paraphernalia and a superb selection of unusual chocolates and confectionery.

98 MONMOUTH COFFEE

27 Monmouth St
WC2H 9EU
Covent Garden ⓘ
+44 (0)20 7232 3010
www.monmouthcoffee.co.uk

Monmouth was founded on this site in 1978, roasting carefully selected imported beans in the basement. They can be credited with pioneering good quality coffee in London at a time when it was only available from a few Italian cafes. They still roast their own beans, sourced from fair trade single-estate farms around the world.

99 FLAT WHITE

17 Berwick St
W1F 0PT
Soho ①
+44 (0)20 7734 0370
www.flatwhitesoho.co.uk

Flat White seeks to bring the refined, artisan style of antipodean coffee to London. Their signature coffee is deliciously creamy: a strong shot of espresso with not-too-hot textured milk poured on top. Sister cafe Milk Bar in Bateman St a few blocks away has more space and a stylish vibe.

100 PRUFROCK

23-25 Leather Lane
EC1N 7TE
Clerkenwell ②
+44 (0)20 7242 0467
www.prufrockcoffee.com

This large open-plan cafe has won the Best Independent Coffee Shop in Europe award and has a reputation for experimenting to find the best production methods. They run the London Barista Resource and Training Centre from the two-floor premises, from where you can graduate with a diploma in coffee making.

97 ALGERIAN COFFEE STORES

5 coffee shops
TO WATCH
THE WORLD GO BY

---

101 BAR ITALIA
22 Frith St
W1D 4RF
Soho ①
+44 (0)20 7437 4520
www.baritaliasoho.co.uk

Bar Italia is a wonderful survival from the heady days of 1950s Soho. It retains a real old-school charm, as well as a Gaggia machine and original mechanical till. It was opened in 1949 and is still run by the same family. Open from 7 am to 5 am it's a great place to come late at night, as memorialised in the Pulp song of the same name.

102 COFFEE PLANT
180 Portobello Road
W11 2EB
West ⑦
+44 (0)20 8453 1144
www.coffee.uk.com

A community-hub cafe in Notting Hill's Portobello Road with an alternative and arty vibe, and a rather basic décor. Sit in the window or outside on the street to watch the market traders, tourists and locals going about their business.

103 ST JAMES'S CAFE
St James's Park
SW1A 2BJ
South West ⑥
+44 (0)207 839 1149

In the middle of St James's Park in central London this cafe is perfectly located for a relaxing coffee amongst the quiet trees and greenery. The building, with its wooden organic geometry, is very elegant and fits beautifully into the landscape.

104 NUDE ESPRESSO

25 Hanbury Street
E1 6QR
East ③
+44 (0)78 0422 3590
www.nudeespresso.com

Nude's new open-spaced cafe is in a warehouse-like room that houses their micro-roastery, right opposite their original cafe. The huge windows offer great views of passers-by in this creative area, full of interesting independent shops.

105 CLIMPSON & SONS

67 Broadway Market
E8 4PH
Hackney ⑨
+44 (0)20 7812 9829
www.climpsonandsons.com

This popular cafe has a good view onto one of London's hippest enclaves. At the weekend, when the street market is open, it gets very busy, but come in the week for a more relaxed experience. This area has an arty, creative and enterprising vibe. The people-watching here is great.

The 5 best
ROOFTOP DRINKING SPOTS

---

106 DALSTON ROOF PARK

The Print House
18-22 Ashwin St
E8 3DL
Hackney ⑨
+44 (0)20 7275 0825

Inspired by New York's High Line Project this east London rooftop park opens each summer for film screenings, music events, yoga and drinking. It features a garden area with a bar and street food stalls. The four-storey building has impressive views of the London skyline. Run by the innovative Bootstrap Company it houses affordable community workspaces, and is a utopian urban oasis.

107 BOUNDARY ROOFTOP BAR

2-4 Boundary St
Entrance: Redchurch St
E2 7DD
East ③
+44 (0)20 7729 1051
www.theboundary.co.uk/ rooftop

Located in the heart of Shoreditch this rooftop bar is part of the Terence Conran designed Boundary project, which also includes a design hotel and a restaurant. The excellent Albion shop and cafe on the ground floor specialises in modern British food. The rooftop is open all year round and has a garden, bar area and canopied restaurant. The panoramic views are impressive, especially at night.

108 **FRANK'S CAFE**
Peckham Multi-Storey
Carpark
10th floor
95A Rye Lane
SE15 4ST
South ⑤
+44 (0)20 7928 3850
www.frankscafe.org.uk

Occupying the roof of a ten-floor disused multi-storey carpark in Peckham, this cafe and bar is open in the summer months. The cafe is part of a wider artistic project run by Bold Tendencies, which uses the rest of the carpark for art installations, theatre, music, film screenings and events. On a sunny evening it's a fantastic place to be, with a great vibe.

109 **PROOF**
Field Works
Martello St
E8 3QW
Hackney ⑨
www.playground
andproof.com

Open all year round this rooftop bar in London Fields is a hipster favourite. Amongst the treetops there's a curved wooden terrace with a bar and the space also hosts special events and film screenings. On the ground level there's a daytime street food market called Playground.

110 **QUEEN ELIZABETH HALL ROOF GARDEN**
South Bank Centre
Belvedere Road
SE1 8XX
Southbank ④
+44 (0)20 7960 4200

Part of the Southbank Centre complex, this wonderful roof garden is hidden away but easily accessed from the river embankment. It's an unexpected delight amongst the brutalist stonework with, in the summer months, a cafe and bar. It's a great place to watch the sun set right in the heart of London.

The 5 best
COCKTAIL BARS

---

111 **MARK'S BAR**
AT HIX SOHO
66-70 Brewer St
W1F 9UP
Soho ①
+44 (0)20 7292 3518
*www.marksbar.co.uk/
thebars*

A plush, old-school drinking den with a warm and dimly-lit ambiance. It appears civilised, but this place encourages decadence. The unusual cocktail list is informed by a centuries old history of British drinking tradition with one section named 'Early British Libations'. Sit at the long bar if you want to enjoy the theatre of preparing a Zombie or Shipwreck Blazer.

112 **HAPPINESS FORGETS**
8-9 Hoxton Square
N1 6NU
East ③
+44 (0)20 7613 0325
www.happinessforgets.com

Easy to miss at street level, this tiny candlelit bar offers 'high end cocktails in a low rent basement.' Known as a bartenders' bar, the cocktails here are as innovative and inventive as the décor is low-key and understated.

113 **NIGHTJAR**
129 City Road
EC1V 1JB
East ③
+44 (0)20 7253 4101
www.barnightjar.com

This prohibition-style bar in Shoreditch has a great vibe with live jazz and swing music every night after 9. The creative cocktail list is divided into historic eras; pre-prohibition, prohibition, post-war and Nightjar signatures. This is a busy spot, so book ahead.

114 SATAN'S WHISKERS

343 Cambridge Heath
Road
E2 9RA
East ③
+44 (0)20 7739 8362

Outside it may resemble a dive bar, with a tiny pink neon sign advertising the enticing name, but inside there's a more salubrious and quirky bar area which is heavy on the taxidermy. The signature drink features gin, vermouth, Grand Marnier, bitters and orange juice. The soundtrack is old-school hip-hop.

115 AMERICAN BAR

AT THE SAVOY
100 Strand
WC2R 0EZ
Covent Garden ①
+44 (0)20 7836 4343
www.fairmont.com/savoy-london/dining/americanbar

Hidden inside the stately Savoy Hotel the American Bar opened in 1893 and was the first in Europe to import the popular US style of mixed liquors. It's a place of legend where Harry Craddock invented many now-classic cocktails. There's a jazz-age art deco feel here, polished and elegant, with live piano every evening.

111 MARK'S BAR

The 5 best
WINE BARS

---

116 GORDON'S WINE BAR

47 Villiers St
WC2N 6NE
Covent Garden ①
+44 (0)20 7930 1408
www.gordonswinebar.com

London's oldest wine bar opened in 1890 in a building where writers Samuel Pepys (1680s) and Rudyard Kipling (1890s) once lived. It feels older still, occupying a catacomb-like cellar space – incredibly atmospheric with candles, rickety tables and yellowing newsprint on the bare brick walls.

117 NOBLE ROT

51 Lamb's Conduit St
WC1N 3NB
Bloomsbury ②
+44 (0)20 7242 8963
*www.noblerot.co.uk/
wine-bar*

This characterful and grown-up Parisian-style wine bar and restaurant was recently opened by the excellent wine and food magazine of the same name, and channels its colourful and punkish spirit. The wine list is multi award-winning and the food is seriously good Franglaise style.

118 TERROIRS

5 William IV St
WC2N 4DW
Covent Garden ①
+44 (0)20 7036 0660
www.terroirswinebar.com

The focus of the wine list here is on small scale, artisan producers who use traditional methods to make biodynamic and organic wines. The food is rustic French with a British and Spanish twist, with interesting small plates.

119 **BAR PEPITO**

3 Varnishers Yard
N1 9FD
Bloomsbury ②
+44 (0)20 7841 7331
www.barpepito.co.uk

Pepito is a tiny sherry bar. All the delicious wood-aged Spanish wines from Jerez are here: Manzanilla, Fino, Amontillado and Pedro Ximinez. From the very driest to the sweetest sherry, there's incredible variety on offer. They serve good tapas and offer a 'Caminito de Pepito' – a six-course tasting menu matching food with wine.

120 **ANTIDOTE WINE BAR**

12A Newburgh St
W1F 7RR
Soho ①
+44 (0)20 7287 8488
www.antidotewinebar.com

Antidote has a casual and lively ground floor bar and a more formal restaurant upstairs. The wine list is largely French, featuring many small and interesting producers. Plenty of wines are available to try by the glass and can be paired with the small plates and charcuterie on offer.

120 ANTIDOTE WINEBAR

The 5 best places for a
CUP OF TEA

---

121 **YAUATCHA**
15-17 Broadwick St
W1F 0DL
Soho ①
+44 (0)20 7494 8888
www.yauatcha.com/soho/
tea-at-yauatcha

Yauatcha is well known for its dim sum and wonderful loose leaf teas, of which there are more than 40 sourced from China and India. Afternoon tea is served with Chinese savoury delicacies. You can also take your tea with an exquisite range of patisserie, macarons and petits gateaux.

122 **AMANZI**
24 New Cavendish St
W1G 8TX
Marylebone ⑧
+44 (0)20 7935 5510
www.amanzitea.com

This modern Marylebone teahouse offers a mind-bending selection of teas with 150 premium loose leaf teas to choose from and almost as many different ways to drink them. There are chais, lattes, frappés, bubble teas, fruit infusions and virgin cocktail teas.

123 **SKETCH**
9 Conduit St
W1S 2XG
Mayfair ⑧
+44 (0)20 7659 4500
www.sketch.london

Sketch is a high-concept restaurant and tearoom that undoubtedly has some of the best décor in London. Take their afternoon tea in The Gallery, a sumptuous low-lit pink room with unsettling humorous artworks by David Shrigley. There's excellent service and a fun atmosphere.

124 POSTCARD TEAS

9 Dering St
W1S 1AG
Mayfair ⑧
+44 (0)20 7629 3654
www.postcardteas.com/site

One of the best places to buy tea in town. All 60 varieties, beautifully packaged, are fairly traded from small single estate farms. Real expertise has gone into creating and importing the selection available. They also sell postcards, filled with loose tea, which you can send anywhere in the world.

125 FORTNUM & MASON

181 Piccadilly
W1A 1ER
Mayfair ⑧
+44 (0)20 7734 8040
www.fortnumandmason.com

This landmark establishment on Piccadilly takes its tea very seriously and has done so for more than 300 years. A huge range of high quality teas are available, immaculately packaged in their signature *eau de nil bleu* and gold livery. For the quintessential English tearoom experience the Diamond Jubilee Tea Salon is the place to come.

123 SKETCH

The 5 best
CYCLE CAFES

---

126 RAPHA CYCLE CLUB LONDON

85 Brewer St
W1F 9ZN
Soho ①
+44 (0)20 7494 9831
www.pages.rapha.cc/clubs/london

Rapha has become something of a cult amongst road cyclists lately, and this stylish London HQ is the place to come if you want to see the entire range of their high-end clothing in one place. Head into the cafe area where TV screens show live cycle racing. The glass-topped tables have vintage cycling memorabilia on display.

127 LOOK MUM NO HANDS!

49 Old St
EC1V 9HX
Clerkenwell ②
+44 (0)20 7253 1025
www.lookmumnohands.com

LMNH was one of the first cycle cafes and it's still one of the best. The cafe is excellent, providing coffee, fresh food, pastries and craft ales. There's a workshop for repairs and they sell a branded range of caps, socks, tees and jerseys. During the Tour de France LMNH is *en fête* – it's the best place to come and watch the racing.

128 SOHO BIKES

26 Berwick St
W1F 8RG
Soho ①
+44 (0)20 7439 9577
www.sohobikes.co.uk

At the front of this narrow bike shop is a small cafe area serving great coffee from Shoreditch roasters Ozone and hearty, healthy food with a screen to watch any racing that might be on. There's also a workshop for repairs and wheel and bike building.

129 CYCLELAB & JUICEBAR

16B-18A Pitfield St
N1 6EY
East ③
+44 (0)20 3222 0016
www.cyclelabuk.
wordpress.com

This Shoreditch bike shop has an excellent range of bikes, accessories and clothing for sale, a workshop for repairs and servicing and it even offers yoga classes specially tailored for cyclists. The cafe serves locally roasted Square Mile coffee, fresh juices, smoothies and plenty of good food. They even have a custom-built bike that produces smoothies as you pedal.

130 CADENCE PERFORMANCE

2A Anerley Hill
SE19 2AA
South ⑤
+44 (0)20 8676 8825
www.cadence
performance.com

The aim of this centre is to improve a cyclist's riding performance by offering bike fittings, training programmes, fitness testing, coaching and nutritional advice. There's a great cafe for filling up on artisan coffee, cakes and energy bars.

126 RAPHA CYCLE CLUB LONDON

The 5 best
PUBS for REAL ALE

———

131 THE HARP
47 Chandos Place
WC2N 4HS
Covent Garden ①
+44 (0)20 7836 0291
www.harpcoventgarden.com

This attractive little pub has a pretty exterior with stained glass windows and flowers cascading from hanging baskets. Inside there's a friendly atmosphere and a fantastic ever-changing selection of at least 10 real ales on tap at any time, as well as a good cider and perry selection. It's the only London pub to win the Campaign For Real Ale's National Pub of the Year award.

132 THE JERUSALEM TAVERN
55 Britton St
EC1M 5UQ
Clerkenwell ②
+44 (0)20 7490 4281
*www.stpetersbrewery.
co.uk/london-pub*

Occupying a 1790 building this pub is owned by the St Peter's Brewery in Suffolk. In a moated hall in the countryside they produce more than 20 high quality traditional ales including Best, Mild and Golden on cask and IPA, Ruby Porter and Spelt Blonde in bottles. It's a special pub with a warm atmosphere.

133 **WENLOCK ARMS**

26 Wenlock Road
N1 7TA
East ③
+44 (0)20 7608 3406
www.wenlockarms.com

This traditional street-corner pub, only recently saved from developers, has been serving ales since 1836. There's a constantly changing selection of 10 real ales on tap, as well as 7 ciders and a number of craft ales. They offer a fuss-free menu of quality bar snacks and salt beef sandwiches.

134 **THE MARKET PORTER**

9 Stoney St
Borough Market
SE1 9AA
Southbank ④
+44 (0)20 7407 2495

The Market Porter is named after the workers who ported food and goods around Borough Market, which is right on the doorstep of this pub. It still opens from 6-8.30 am in the mornings to serve the market trade. They have at least 10 different marques of ale at any time and Harveys's Sussex Best is an ever-present.

135 **JOLLY BUTCHERS**

204 Stoke Newington
High St
N16 7HU
Hackney ⑨
+44 (0)20 7249 9471
www.jollybutchers.co.uk

This relatively new pub in Stoke Newington is a fantastic all-rounder. Not only does it serve an excellent range of real ales from Britain's best independent brewers, it also offers craft beers, premium lagers and bottled beers from all over the world.

The 5 best pubs for a
RIVERSIDE DRINK

---

136 **THE DOVE**
19 Upper Mall
W6 9TA
West ⑦
+44 (0)20 8748 9474
www.dovehammersmith.
co.uk

This early 18th-century pub, cosy and low-ceilinged, is right on the Thames and accessed from a narrow path past Hammersmith Bridge. Close to the front door is a tiny room with seating for only a couple of people – this is claimed to be the smallest bar room in the world. There are excellent river views from the back of the pub.

137 **TAMESIS DOCK**
Albert Embankment
SE1 7TP
Southbank ④
+44 (0)20 7582 1066
www.tdock.co.uk

This brightly painted converted Dutch barge is a floating pub, moored on the Albert Embankment between Vauxhall and Lambeth Bridges. It enjoys wonderful river views across the Thames to the Houses of Parliament and Big Ben, best seen from the open-air top deck.

138 THE PROSPECT OF WHITBY

57 Wapping Wall
E1W 3SH
East ③
+44 (0)20 7481 1095

Dating from 1520 the Prospect claims to be London's oldest riverside pub. It has excellent views of the Thames and was a former haunt of smugglers, thieves and pirates as well as 'hanging' Judge Jeffries, who sentenced many to die at nearby Execution Dock. A noose hangs from a scaffold in the river to commemorate this history. Charles Dickens and Samuel Pepys are known to have drunk here.

139 FOUNDERS ARMS

52 Hopton St
Bankside
SE1 9JH
Southbank ④
+44 (0)20 7928 1899
www.foundersarms.co.uk

Right on the Thames Path and next to Tate Modern this contemporary pub has a great position by the river, with impressive views from the large garden terrace and full-length pub windows across to St Paul's Cathedral and the City. Young's ales and gastro-pub dishes are served.

140 THE ANGEL

101 Bermondsey Wall East
SE16 4NB
Southbank ④
+44 (0)20 7394 3214

This Victorian pub in Rotherhithe has an outside balcony and views from both floors across the Thames to the skyscrapers of the City and upstream to Tower Bridge. Behind the pub are the ruined remains of King Edward III's Manor House, built around 1530. Walk along the Thames Path from Tower Bridge to get here: the views are excellent all the way.

The 5 best places for
CRAFT ALE

---

141 **EUSTON TAP**

190 Euston Road
NW1 2EF
Bloomsbury ②
+44 (0)20 3137 8837
www.eustontap.com

This beer house is located in an unusual building – a Victorian railway gatehouse with ornate classical features. Over 150 bottles and up to 30 taps and kegs are on offer – an exotic array of different styles from independent breweries across the UK, Europe and USA. The Cider Tap is in a similar building opposite.

142 **THE RAKE**

14a Winchester Walk
Borough Market
SE1 9AG
Southbank ④
+44 (0)20 7407 0557
*www.utobeer.co.uk/
the-rake*

The Rake is an intimate craft beer den housed in a former greasy spoon cafe on the margins of Borough Market. It's run by Utobeer, specialist beer importers with a stall at Borough stocking 700 different beers. There are a mere 130 bottles available here, in addition to the 10 or so beers available on keg or cask at any time. Staff are friendly and helpful and the walls are covered in the graffiti of beer makers.

143 CRAFT BEER CO.

82 Leather Lane
EC1N 7TR
Clerkenwell ②
+44 (0)20 7404 7049
www.thecraftbeerco.com/
pubs/clerkenwell

The Craft Beer Co. is a small London chain of specialist craft beer bars. Here you will find one of the largest selections available in town with 400 bottles available and several dozen beers on cask and keg. The knowledgeable staff will help you navigate the menu. A must-visit for hop-heads.

144 THE EXMOUTH ARMS

23 Exmouth Market
EC1R 4QL
Clerkenwell ②
+44 (0)20 3551 4772
www.exmoutharms.com

This handsome Victorian pub in the appealing Exmouth Market area has a hugely impressive beer offering. More than 60 international bottled beers are available, plus a large ever-changing selection of beers on cask. On draught they sell a dozen regular beers including the Camden Brewery range and Bermondsey's Anspach and Hobday.

145 THE DOVETAIL

9-10 Jerusalem Passage
EC1V 4JP
Clerkenwell ②
+44 (0)20 7490 7321
www.dovepubs.com/
aboutdovetail

A bar specialising in Belgian beer, with more than 100 beers available by bottle, including Trappist, saison, fruit, amber and blonde varieties, and 12 more are available on draught. They also serve classic Belgian dishes to help line the stomach.

The 5 best
CRAFT ALE BREWERIES
with a bar

---

146 FOURPURE
BERMONDSEY TRADING
ESTATE
22 Rotherhithe New
Road
SE16 3LL
Southbank ④
+44 (0)20 3744 2141
www.fourpure.com

Founded in 2013 the Fourpure Brewery operates from an industrial estate in South Bermondsey. On Saturdays, from 11 to 5, it opens up a tap room to serve the public directly. They brew high quality US-style craft beers including Session IPA, Pale Ale, Amber Ale and seasonal offerings. It attracts a knowledgeable and enthusiastic crowd of beer aficionados and drinkers.

147 REDCHURCH BREWERY TAP ROOM
275-276 Poyser St
E2 9RF
East ③
+44 (0)20 3487 0255
www.theredchurch brewery.com

Redchurch Brewery was founded in 2011 in Bethnal Green and produces a fine range of craft ales including Bethnal Pale Ale, Hoxton Stout and experimental one-off brews that may include the use of foraged ingredients, such as their Wild Isolation. The Tap Room opened in 2014 above the brewery. Their full range of beers are available and there are often DJs and live music.

148 **BEAVERTOWN BREWERY**
Units 2, 17 & 18
Lockwood Industrial
Park
Mill Mead Road
N17 9QP
Hackney ⑨
+44 (0)20 8525 9884
*www.beavertownbrewery.
co.uk*

Beavertown in Tottenham Hale was founded in 2012 and has since won much acclaim, with head brewer Jenn Merrick being awarded British Guild of Beer Writers' Brewer of the Year 2015. The tap room, open on Saturdays from 2 to 8, is where you'll be able to try all the regular favourites such as Gamma Ray Pale Ale and one-off brews such as the Armagnac Barrel Aged Moose Fang.

149 **PARTIZAN BREWING**
8 Almond Road
SE16 3LR
Southbank ④
+44 (0)20 8127 5053
*www.partizanbrewing.
co.uk*

If you're exploring the Bermondsey Beer Mile from Maltby Street Market then the Partizan Brewery will be one of your port of calls. The bar is open on Saturdays from 11 – 5. Beers include Real Time Saison Pale Ale and Lemongrass Saison. Admire their fantastic graphic label designs as you stand among the empty hop pallets in the alley.

150 **CAMDEN TOWN BREWERY BAR**
55-59 Wilkin Street
Mews
NW5 3NN
North ⑩
+44 (0)20 7485 1671
*www.camdentown
brewery.com*

Camden Town Brewery produces its beers from under some Victorian railway arches, one of which contains a bar that opens from Tuesday to Sunday. The complete range of beers are available here on tap, and various limited and special runs.

The 5 best
SOHO BOOZERS

---

151 GLASSHOUSE STORES

55 Brewer St
W1F 9UL
Soho ⓘ
+44 (0)20 7287 5278

This Victorian pub has a lovely wooden bar and interior and an old-time atmosphere, with nicotine-stained walls. It's a Sam Smith's pub and sells the full range of the Yorkshire brewer's beers at great value prices. The only Soho pub to have a bar billiards table, it also has a downstairs bar room open in the evenings and serves good, if basic, pub food.

152 THE FRENCH HOUSE

49 Dean St
W1D 5BG
Soho ⓘ
+44 (0)20 7437 2477
www.frenchhousesoho.com

The French House is a unique pub and a real Soho institution that occupies a Grade II listed building over two rather cramped floors. There's no music, no TV or any machines and mobile phones are banned here – this is a place that encourages conversation. It has long attracted Soho's more bohemian crowd of actors, writers, artists and bons viveurs. Regulars have included Francis Bacon, Dylan Thomas and Lucien Freud. Beers are only served in half pint measures.

152 THE FRENCH HOUSE

153 THE COACH AND HORSES

29 Greek St
W1D 5DH
Soho ①
+44 (0)20 7437 5920
*www.thecoachandhorses
soho.co.uk*

This pub's place in Soho drinking legend is secure thanks to Norman Balon, a former landlord with a reputation for rudeness, and columnist Jeffrey Bernard, whose Low Life column in The Spectator catalogued the goings-on here. Now London's only vegetarian pub, and still a favourite with writers and journalists, it hosts regular piano singalongs on Wednesday and Sunday evenings.

154 THE LYRIC

37 Great Windmill St
W1D 7LU
Soho ①
+44 (0)20 7434 0604
www.lyricsoho.co.uk

Unusually for Soho this attractive little pub near Theatreland has an excellent beer selection with more than 20 beers available on tap including craft ales from The Kernel and Beavertown breweries. The interiors over the two floors are full of character with painted tiles, wooden features and open fires.

155 THE BLUE POSTS

22 Berwick St
W1F 0QA
Soho ①
+44 (0)20 7437 5008

Perhaps the most old-school boozer still going in Soho, the Blue Posts has a basic interior which is not without its own charm. 'Blue posts' are said to have been used for demarcating royal hunting grounds, which might explain why there are so many pubs of the same name in this area, which was once a hunting ground. The Soho area is named after a hunting call.

5

PUBS *with* AMAZING INTERIORS

---

156 THE PRINCESS LOUISE
208 High Holborn
WC1V 7EP
Bloomsbury ②
+44 (0)20 7405 8816
*www.princesslouisepub.
co.uk*

A fine example of a 19th-century 'gin palace' this large hostelry has one of the most spectacularly ornate pub interiors in London. It dates from 1891 and is very well preserved with original features including panelled wooden booths, bevelled glass, a circular bar and mosaic tiling. The whole building is listed for its historic merit with the men's toilets having a special listing of their own for their incredible monumental marble fittings.

157 THE OLD BANK OF ENGLAND
194 Fleet St
EC4A 2LT
City ④
+44 (0)20 7430 2255
*www.oldbankofengland.
co.uk*

This unusual pub occupies an imposing Grade I listed 1888 building which was once a branch of the Bank of England. The Crown Jewels and gold bullion were once stored in the vaults. The main bar room is hugely impressive and grand, with incredibly high ceilings, tall windows, raised galleries and an abundance of dark wood.

158 THE CHAMPION

12-13 Wells St
W1T 3PA
Soho ①
+44 (0)20 7323 1228

The Champion is notable for its highly unusual stained glass windows, which beautifully depict British sporting heroes and eminences of the Victorian period. These include cricketer WG Grace, mountaineer Edward Whymper, channel swimmer Matthew Webb and Florence Nightingale.

159 THE BLACKFRIAR

174 Queen Victoria St
EC4V 4EG
City ④
+44 (0)20 7236 5474

This unique pub stands on the site of the 13th-century Blackfriars monastery. The ecclesiastical history is richly portrayed on seemingly every surface of the interior, decorated in the early 20th century by designers associated with the Arts and Crafts movement. They really went to town on the design, with copper reliefs, mosaics and stone carvings giving a distinctly medieval feel to the place.

160 THE LAMB

94 Lamb's Conduit St
WC1N 3LZ
Bloomsbury ②
+44 (0)20 7405 0713
www.thelamblondon.com

Named after George Lamb, who erected a water conduit here in 1577, this Bloomsbury pub was built in the 1720s with the interiors dating from the Victorian period. It's one of only a few pubs to have surviving 'snob screens,' which were made of wood and etched glass and designed to give privacy to courting gentlemen at the bar.

The 5 best places for a
FUN NIGHT OUT

---

161 **BETHNAL GREEN WORKING MENS' CLUB**
42-44 Pollard Row
E2 6NB
East ③
+44 (0)20 7739 7170
www.workersplaytime.net

An authentic East End working men's club that dates back to 1953, hidden on a Bethnal Green backstreet. A huge range of live music, comedy, cabaret, burlesque and club night events are on offer here that tend towards the racy, wild and occasionally unhinged.

162 **HORSE MEAT DISCO**
AT: EAGLE LONDON
349 Kennington Lane
SE11 5QY
Southbank ④
+44 (0)20 7793 0903
www.eaglelondon.com/horse-meat-disco

A Sunday night institution at Vauxhall's legendary gay venue Eagle London for over 13 years, HMD is inspired by the pioneering nightlife of 1970s New York. An inclusive queer party for everyone that's 'dedicated to the industry of human happiness', the resident DJs play obscure underground and classic disco and are frequently joined by some of the world's finest disco selectors.

163 BAR KICK

127 Shoreditch High St
E1 6JE
East ③
+44 (0)20 7739 8700
www.cafekick.co.uk/bar-kick

This attractive continental-style table football bar has original French Bonzini tables with cast-iron figurines and is decorated with colourful flags and old posters. It's the venue for the prestigious London Table Football Championship. Exmouth Market is home to a smaller version called Cafe Kick.

164 KANSAS SMITTY'S

63-65 Broadway Market
E8 4PH
Hackney ⑨
+44 (0)7731 016 744
www.kansassmittys.com

Smitty's is an intimate subterranean jazz bar and tribute to Kansas City's anti-prohibition bebop scene. The cocktail list is based on Southern juleps and bourbon. The bar was set up by the house band, a crack set of young musicians who regularly appear at Ronnie Scott's. When they're not on stage, DJs play a lively mix of swing, 50s R&B and hard bop jazz. The place can get noisy and crackles with energy.

165 EFES SNOOKER CLUB

17B Stoke Newington
Road
N16 8BH
Hackney ⑨
+44 (0)20 7249 6040

A Turkish pool and snooker hall in Dalston, Efes is a rough and ready drinking place that's popular with young hipsters. Kitsch murals adorn the walls and the pool tables are well-used. They've recently started hosting mini-golf tournaments around the space too, and occasionally host club nights.

COMMERCIAL IRON WORKS.

KICK

163 **BAR KICK**

Welcome to EFES

165 **EFES SNOOKER CLUB**

MAGMA

75 PLACES
TO SHOP

---

5 shops for
BRITISH DESIGN

166 **CUBITTS**
37 Marshall St
W1F 7EZ
Soho ①
+44 (0)20 7129 8128
www.cubitts.co.uk

Cubitts make elegant handmade spectacles and sunglasses for men and women. All the models are named after London streets such as Judd, Brunswick, Calthorpe and Marchmont. The glasses are modestly priced given their quality and the 50 separate design processes involved.

167 **UNTO THIS LAST**
230 Brick Lane
E2 7EB
East ③
+44 (0)20 7613 0882
www.untothislast.co.uk

An innovative and forward-thinking contemporary furniture maker, named after a John Ruskin essay that advocated a return to local craftsmanship in the industrial age. This Brick Lane workshop is also a shop window for their plywood designs. They offer the convenience and skill of a local workshop at affordable prices.

168 JASPER MORRISON SHOP

24B Kingsland Road
E2 8DA
East ③
www.jaspermorrisonshop.
com

Industrial designer Jasper Morrison is known for his every-day, useful designs of household products. This discreetly located small showroom in Shoreditch brings together his designs for leading international manufacturers with similarly elegant and utile products from other designers.

169 TIMOROUS BEASTIES

46 Amwell St
EC1R 1XS
Clerkenwell ②
+44 (0)20 7833 5010
www.timorousbeasties.com

Founded by a pair of Glasgow School of Art students and named after a poem by Robert Burns, this tiny and homely store stocks an entire collection of wallpapers, printed fabrics, cushions and ceramic designs. Contemporary subversions of Victorian period tropes, they range from traditional scenes of nature to Rorschachian psychedelia and pure abstraction and pattern.

170 DAVID MELLOR

4 Sloane Square
SW1W 8EE
South West ⑥
+44 (0)20 7730 4259
www.davidmellordesign.
com

This Chelsea kitchenware shop is a showcase for the designs of the late David Mellor and his son Corin. The cutlery, ceramics, glass and accessories are all produced in their Derbyshire factory and share an elegant simplicity. The shop also sells pottery and wood-crafted pieces from a variety of British studios and kindred European designers.

5 *essential*
FASHION SHOPS *for* MEN

171 PRESENT LONDON

140 Shoreditch High St
E1 6JE
East ③
+44 (0)20 7033 0500
www.present-london.com

This stylishly designed boutique has an ever-changing selection of men's fashion. A mixture of heritage brands and innovative new designers includes Vetra, Trickers, William Fox, Gloverall and Creep. The fascia of the shop has retained the signage from a previous incumbent, The Golden Horn Cigarette Company.

172 THE GARBSTORE

188 Kensington Park Road
W11 2ES
West ⑦
+44 (0)20 7229 2178
www.couvertureand thegarbstore.com

The Garbstore in Notting Hill is a showcase for Ian Paley's 'unfamiliar vintage' brand. They also stock a range of kindred international brands and accessories. The upper floors are occupied by womenswear brand Couverture, making this an excellent his-and-hers retail expedition.

173 OI POLLOI

1 Marshall St
W1F 9BA
Soho ①
+44 (0)20 7734 2585
www.oipolloi.com

Oi Polloi recently opened this London outpost of their seminal Manchester boutique, with an essential edit of the full range available in their northern shop. The focus is on quality brand-led casual, sports and heritage clothing.

174 ALBAM

Spitalfields Market
111a Commercial St
E1 6BG
East ③
+44 (0)20 7247 6254
www.albamclothing.com

This small chain of London shops (the others are in Soho and Islington) exclusively sell the Albam range of 'timeless British menswear'. Their designs have an understated elegance that focus on materials and the attention to small details.

175 TRUNK CLOTHIERS

8 Chiltern St
W1U 7PU
Marylebone ⑧
+44 (0)20 7486 2357
www.trunkclothiers.com

This high-end boutique offers a lovingly curated range for gentlemen seeking suits, modern classics and a high level of craftsmanship. A few doors along from the main shop is the Trunk Lab which sells only accessories such as handkerchiefs, luggage, grooming products, homewares and stationery.

171 PRESENT LONDON

5 essential
FASHION SHOPS
for WOMEN

---

176 WONDEROUND
16 Calvert Avenue
E2 7JP
East ③
www.wonderound.co.uk

Taking its name from the idea of 'wonderful things around you' this small boutique and lifestyle store is packed with clothes, accessories and gift ideas that have an uncomplicated elegance. The simple and comfortable clothes are from unusual international designers that you won't find anywhere else.

177 MARGARET HOWELL
34 Wigmore St
W1U 2RS
Marylebone ⑧
+44 (0)20 7009 9009
www.margarethowell.co.uk

This beautiful store is the flagship of the Margaret Howell business and the location for her design studio. The clothes have a timeless appeal and an emphasis on functionality, high quality fabrics and craftsmanship. There's also an interesting range of mid-century British design products.

178 THE MERCANTILE
17 Lamb St
E1 6EA
East ③
+44 (0)20 7377 8926
www.themercantile
london.com

This relaxed independent boutique showcases an ever-changing mix of contemporary brands from the UK and abroad including Custommade, Hiro + Wolf and Samsoe & Samsoe. Alongside the clothes is a wide range of gifts, accessories, shoes and apothecary.

179 AIMÉ

17 Redchurch St
E2 7DJ
East ③
+44 (0)20 7739 2158
www.aimelondon.com

A tiny redoubt of Parisian chic in Shoreditch, Aimé is a boutique stocking desirable contemporary French and European designs including those by Isabel Marant, Vanessa Seward and Michel Vivien. The small but inspiring collection of jewellery, gifts, ceramics, plants and cacti adds to the allure.

180 THE KEEP

GRANVILLE ARCADE

32-33 Coldharbour Lane
SW9 8PR
South ⑤
+44 (0)20 7924 0867
www.thekeepboutique.com

Offering a stylish and beautiful range of clothes that you'll want to keep, this Brixton Village boutique sources ethical fashion from around the globe. Brands include Here Today Here Tomorrow, Komodo, The People Tree and Quazi Design. As well as the clothes there's a range of beauty products, aromatherapy oils, homewares and jewellery from Kathmandu.

The 5 best shops for
VINTAGE CLOTHING

---

181 THE VINTAGE SHOWROOM
14 Earlham St
WC2H 9LN
Covent Garden ①
+44 (0)20 7836 3964
www.thevintageshowroom.
com/blog

Housed in a former ironmongery shop near Seven Dials is this unique resource for men's vintage clothing. The stock is well organised and specialises in workwear, military, naval, sports, classic tailoring and country attire from the early to mid-20th century. They've recently published a visual reference book.

182 BEYOND RETRO
92-100 Stoke Newington
Road
N16 7XB
Hackney ⑨
+44 (0)20 7729 9001
www.beyondretro.com/en

This large store in Hackney is the flagship for the Beyond Retro brand, with smaller branches in Soho and Brick Lane. There's every chance you'll find a bargain you didn't realise you needed. An on-site cafe serves refreshments from vintage tea sets.

183 BLACKOUT II
51 Endell St
WC2H 9AJ
Covent Garden ①
+44 (0)20 7240 5006
www.blackout2.com

For nearly 30 years and from well before vintage clothing became the trend it is today, Blackout has offered affordable, high-end vintage fashions for men and women. The heaving stock is spread over two floors and is organised by period, covering the 1920s to 1980s.

184 282 PORTOBELLO

282 Portobello Road
W10 5TE
West ⑦
+44 (0)20 8993 4162
www.282portobello.london

282 is packed with stock that often spills out onto the pavement when the weather allows. The focus is on classic vintage styles that portray a particular English sartorial elegance. The leathers, tweeds, wax jackets, furs, ball gowns and the huge array of footwear, hats and bags attract a bohemian crowd.

185 MINT VINTAGE

71-73 Stoke Newington
High St
N16 8EL
Hackney ⑨
+44 (0)20 7249 4567
www.mintvintage.co.uk

James Wright's store has been at the forefront of trend-driven vintage fashion for a decade now. Originally located in Covent Garden, Mint has now moved out east to the Dalston and Stoke Newington borders, following their hipster clientele. The shop offers an excellent edit of fashion-forward men's and women's clothing with plenty of denim and casualwear.

181 THE VINTAGE SHOWROOM

5 unusual
SPECIALIST SHOPS

---

186 ALICE THROUGH THE LOOKING GLASS

14 Cecil Court
WC2N 4HE
Covent Garden ①
+44 (0)20 7836 8854
www.alicelooking.co.uk

One of the many bookish delights hiding away in historic Cecil Court is this small shop devoted to Lewis Carroll's much loved Alice character. There are hundreds of out of print editions of *Alice's Adventures in Wonderland* and *Alice Through The Looking Glass* with countless different illustrators. They also sell original illustrations, chess sets, chocolates, ceramics, t-shirts and anything else related to the theme.

187 GET STUFFED

105 Essex Road
N1 2SL
Islington ⑪
+44 (0)20 7226 1364
www.thegetstuffed.co.uk

London's leading taxidermy centre is a long-running family business with the most amazing and improbable menagerie on display. The shop is open by appointment only, but most of the stock can be viewed through the windows. As well as the often bizarre animals on show they can also preserve your pet, should you desire.

188 ARTHUR BEALE

194 Shaftesbury Avenue
WC2H 8JP
Covent Garden ①
+44 (0)20 7836 9034
www.arthurbeale.co.uk

This 400-year-old boat chandlery business has been a fixture on Shaftesbury Avenue for 120 years. Stock includes everything from ropes, hooks, bells, barometers and flags to ships biscuits, binoculars, books, life jackets and enamelware. They are also one of the very few places in London to stock the Breton clothing brand St James.

189 RAY MAN MUSIC

54 Chalk Farm Road
NW1 8AN
North ⑩
+44 (0)20 7692 6261
www.raymaneasternmusic.co.uk

Ray Man specialises in drums and percussion from Africa, Asia, the Middle East and South America. Whether you are looking for finger bells, kalimba, woodblocks, nipple gongs, pentatonic balaphones, ocarinas or even dulcimers and zithers, this is the place to come. There are plenty of small and cheap instruments including Vietnamese frog boxes, tam tams, cymbals, shakers and rain sticks that are perfect for an impulse purchase.

190 SYLVANIAN FAMILIES

68 Mountgrove Road
N5 2LT
Islington ⑪
+44 (0)20 7226 1329
www.sylvanian storekeepers.com

This is the only shop in Europe that exclusively sells the anthropomorphic figurines and woodland fixtures that make up the wholesome and charming world of Sylvanian Families. Regular customers know the staff by the names of their Sylvanian alter-egos. Making a pilgrimage here will have to do until you've saved up to visit the theme park in Japan.

The 5 best record shops for
NEW VINYL

**191 SOUNDS OF
THE UNIVERSE**

7 Broadwick St
W1F 0DA
Soho ①
+44 (0)20 7734 3430
*www.soundsoftheuniverse.
com*

Soho has lost many record shops in the
past decade or so, but one of the very
best thankfully remains. SOTU is the
place to go for reggae, Afro, Brazilian,
jazz, underground house and electronica,
as well as for soul, soundtracks and much
more. They run the exemplary Soul Jazz
reissue label, and also sell CDs, music
books and secondhand vinyl.

192 ROUGH TRADE EAST

Old Truman Brewery
91 Brick Lane
E1 6QL
East ③
+44 (0)20 7392 7788
www.roughtrade.com

This large new store off Brick Lane has
an excellent across-the-board selection
that takes in indie, rock, multiple dance
styles, 'world' music and experimental.
There's also a significant and interesting
book selection, a good cafe and a space
that's used for regular free live music
events.

193 PHONICA

51 Poland St
W1F 7LZ
Soho ①
+44 (0)20 7025 6070
www.phonicarecords.com

Phonica has the largest stock of new
electronic and dance music in London.
The main focus is on the various styles of
underground house, techno, bass, disco
and edits but they also cover jazz, reggae,
hip-hop, Balearic, Afro and funk.

194 RYE WAX

The CLF Art Cafe
133 Rye Lane
SE15 4ST
South ⑤
+44 (0)20 7732 3176
www.ryewax.com

Rye Wax is a new opening in Peckham Rye's Bussey Building complex. The stock is focused mainly on house and disco styles. Comics and graphic novels are also on sale and there's a bar and street food pop-up. They regularly host events with DJs, record labels and live artists.

195 HONEST JON'S

278 Portobello Road
W10 5TE
West ⑦
+44 (0)20 8969 9822
www.honestjons.com/shop

Honest Jon's is a West London institution, established in 1974. The carefully selected stock includes reggae, dub, blues, folk, soul, 'outernational' styles, experimental house and techno. They also run an excellent record label that releases pioneering compilations and new artists in diverse, avant-garde styles.

191 SOUNDS OF THE UNIVERSE

The 5 best record shops for
VINTAGE VINYL

196 ELDICA

8 Bradbury St
N16 8JN
Hackney ⑨
+44 (0)20 7254 5220
www.eldica.co.uk

This tiny shop is crammed with mostly black music, especially reggae, soul, funk, jazz, Caribbean and African records, with plenty on 7". The make-up of the stock is partly a reflection of the post-war immigrant communities that were established in this area. It's a digger's delight. They also sell an unusual array of books, ephemera and vintage audio equipment.

197 FLASHBACK

50 Essex Road
N1 8LR
Islington ⑪
+44 (0)20 7354 9356
www.flashback.co.uk

This is the largest branch of what is now a small chain of stores. Upstairs there are CDs and a selection of new vinyl releases. The basement area is vastly bigger and stocks only second hand records, all sensibly priced. The range is truly impressive and you will lose hours in here trying to get through half of it.

198 COSMOS

324D Hackney Road
E2 7AX
East ③
+44 (0)20 7033 8777

One of London's newest record shops is this unusual transplant from Toronto. The unique appeal here is that all of the stock is original vinyl and imported from North America. As a result there are many rare records that are seldom seen on this side of the pond. The stock tends strongly towards the soul, jazz, funk and disco genres, and a little towards the expensive side.

199 LUCKY SEVEN

127 Stoke Newington
Church St
N16 0UH
Hackney ⑨
+44 (0)20 7502 6319

The garish pop shop-front of Lucky 7 stands out on this rapidly gentrifying street. Inside you'll find a huge amount of stock that's crammed to the rafters of this slightly disorderly shop, which also sells old books and magazines. Most of it is available at bargain prices, often for less than a pound an item.

200 MUSIC & VIDEO EXCHANGE

38 Notting Hill Gate
W11 3HL
West ⑦
+44 (0)20 7243 8573
www.mgeshops.com

This is one of the few surviving record shops in the old MVE empire. Stock turns over quickly, aided by the policy of marking down all the prices every month or so. If you take records here you can exchange them for vouchers to spend in the chain's stores, which include a bookshop and vintage clothing shops around the corner.

5 of the best
INDEPENDENT BOOKSHOPS

---

201 LONDON REVIEW BOOKSHOP

14 Bury Place
WC1A 2JL
Bloomsbury ②
+44 (0)20 7269 9030
*www.londonreview
bookshop.co.uk*

This bookshop was set up in 2003 by London Review of Books, the esteemed literary journal. The stock is carefully selected and very strong on literature, biography, politics, history, essays and poetry in particular. They organise several talks and events each month. Through a gap in the wall, between the books, you can access the Cake Shop, which is one of the best cafes in the city, a real literary salon.

202 JOHN SANDOE BOOKS

10 Blacklands Terrace
SW3 2SR
South West ⑥
+44 (0)20 7589 9473
www.johnsandoe.com

Located in recently refurbished and expanded (but still small) premises in an 18th-century terrace, this delightful bookshop is bibliophile's dream. 28.000 titles are crammed in over the three narrow floors, with an emphasis on literature, history, biography, poetry, art and children's. The staff are incredibly knowledgeable and will go the extra mile to find the book you're after.

202 JOHN SANDOE BOOKS

203 LUTYENS & RUBINSTEIN

21 Kensington Park
Road
W11 2EU
West ⑦
+44 (0)20 7229 1010
*www.lutyensrubinstein.
co.uk*

The literature, poetry, children's and art sections are particularly good here, with lots of surprising and excellent selections. The service is expert and friendly. Their innovative A Year in Books is a bespoke service of individually chosen books sent out every month depending on your personal tastes.

204 DAUNT BOOKS

83 Marylebone High St
W1U 4QW
Marylebone ⑧
+44 (0)20 7224 2295
www.dauntbooks.co.uk

Daunt's flagship bookshop is arguably the most beautiful retail space in London, housed in a stunning Edwardian building with oak galleries and skylights. They offer 'books for travellers' – either intellectual or geographical. Their iconic tote bags are something of a fashion accessory around town.

205 FOYLES

107 Charing Cross Road
WC2H 0DT
Soho ①
+44 (0)20 7437 5660
www.foyles.co.uk

Foyles is London's biggest independent bookshop, and probably its most legendary. Founded in 1903 it has recently entered a new and modern era, having moved the flagship store a few doors down the street into a purpose-built 'bookshop of the future.' The new building has an airy atrium, smart cafe, large events space and thankfully Ray's Jazz shop still has its corner niche.

5 of the best
SPECIALIST BOOKSHOPS

206 **ARTWORDS**

20-22 Broadway Market
E8 4QJ
Hackney ⑨
+44 (0)20 7923 7507
www.artwords.co.uk

Artwords specialise in books and magazines that cater to the large number of creatives who work in this area. They have a huge selection of international magazines on contemporary art, fashion, architecture, interiors and design. The books are carefully chosen by the owner and cover the same areas in more depth.

207 **PHOTOGRAPHERS' GALLERY BOOKSHOP**

16-18 Ramillies St
W1F 7LW
Soho ①
+44 (0)20 7087 9300
www.thephotographers gallery.org.uk/bookshop

Located in the basement of the recently built Photographers' Gallery, this excellent bookshop specialises in photographic monographs, anthologies and writing on the subject. The gallery is free to enter before 12 pm and the exhibition programme, including the annual Deutsche Börse Prize, is excellent.

208 STANFORDS

12-14 Long Acre
WC2E 9LP
Covent Garden ①
+44 (0)20 7836 1321
www.stanfords.co.uk

Stanfords is the biggest map and travel bookshop in the world. Founded in 1853 it moved to this flagship site in 1901 and covers three large floors. The depth and range of the stock is amazing, and you will be sure to find inspiration for your future travels.

209 GOSH!

1 Berwick St
W1F 0DR
Soho ①
+44 (0)20 7636 1011
www.goshlondon.com

Gosh! sell a fantastic and expert range of comics, graphic novels, manga and illustrated children's titles. They recently relocated to this attractive new building, covering two floors. Old and new comics are downstairs and the ground floor has the widest range of new graphic titles, from mainstream to cutting edge.

210 PETER HARRINGTON

43 Dover St
W1S 4FF
Mayfair ⑧
+44 (0)20 3763 3220
www.peterharrington.co.uk

This antiquarian and rare book dealer has a welcoming new shop where you can see (and buy) some of the rarest and most expensive books in the world. If you are looking for a Shakespeare First Folio or a first edition of James Joyce's *Ulysses* then this is the place to come. They sell a mix of modern and classic titles (and original illustrations) from the 15th to the 21st centuries.

The 5 best shops for
VINTAGE DESIGN
and HOMEWARES

---

211 **LASSCO**

Ropewalk
41 Maltby St
SE1 3PA
Southbank ④
+44 (0)20 7394 8061
www.lassco.co.uk

Lassco specialise in architectural antiques, industrial salvage and reclaimed flooring. Their range includes doorknobs, chimneys, furniture, lighting, storage, garden ornaments, nauticalia, artworks, textiles and smocks. There are many curiosities and unique pieces. Combine with a trip to Maltby Street Market at the weekend.

212 **MORBLEU**

135 Dulwich Road
SE24 0NG
South ⑤
+44 (0)7958 673 703
www.bleufurniture.com

Located opposite Brockwell Park and the Lido, Morbleu (an archaic exclamation of surprise) specialises in antiques, mid-century and modern vintage furniture, lighting and associated decorative items with an emphasis on retro-industrial and obscure objects. There's a good turnover of stock so you're likely to be pleasantly surprised on each visit.

213 ERNO DECO

328 Portobello Road
W10 5RU
West ⑦
+44 (0)7932 730 827
*www.instagram.com/
ernodeco*

In the shadow of Ernö Goldfinger's iconic Trellick Tower, at the far northern end of Portobello Road, Erno Deco specialises in wild, wonderful and eccentric interior design items, collected from the owner's travels around the globe. It's full of unique, exotic and one-off objects, furniture and textiles from abroad, plus unusual industrial and reclaimed pieces.

214 ATOMIC ANTIQUES

125 Shoreditch High St
E1 6JE
East ③
+44 (0)20 7739 5923
www.atomica.me.uk

This small shop has a carefully selected and high quality range of European and British pieces from the 1920s to the 1980s, with an emphasis on works from the atomic age (mid-century period). They stock period furniture (Hans Wegner, Joe Columbo, Arne Jacobsen), industrial items and decorative works including lighting, ceramics, posters and rugs.

215 FOREST

115 Clerkenwell Road
EC1R 5BY
Clerkenwell ②
+44 (0)20 7242 7370
www.forestlondon.com

A beautifully arranged salesroom with fine examples of original Scandinavian and Dutch mid-century modern period furniture and lighting. The seats, armchairs, tables and cabinets are complimented by an astute selection of German ceramics, prints, mirrors and pot plants.

211 **LASSCO**

214 **ATOMIC ANTIQUES**

215 **FOREST**

5 shops for contemporary
INTERIOR DESIGN

216 **SCP EAST**

135-139 Curtain Road
EC2A 3BX
East ③
+44 (0)20 7739 1869
www.scp.co.uk

SCP started 30 years ago as a furniture-making design company inspired by the Modern Movement. Today they work with leading designers to produce textiles and tableware to complement their furniture. The shop also sells a wide range of design products including lighting, toys, kilims, gifts, books and stationery as well as some vintage pieces.

217 **TWENTYTWENTYONE**

274-275 Upper St
N1 2UA
Islington ⑪
+44 (0)20 7288 1996
www.twentytwentyone.com

As their name suggests, this high-end store specialises in combining 20th-century design and furniture with a progressive selection of innovative 21st-century products. They stock a small range of their own furniture as well as licensed reissues of classic designs by the likes of Eames, Prouvé and Wegner, and a few vintage mid-century pieces.

218 SKANDIUM

35-36 Thurloe Place
SW7 2HP
South West ⑥
+44 (0)20 3876 2744
www.skandium.com

This large store, spread over two floors, presents the very best in classic and contemporary Scandinavian design and furniture. They champion brands such as ittala, Fritz Hansen and Marimekko and designers like Aalvar Aalto, Georg Jensen and Eero Saarinen. There's an amazing array of products that includes furniture, textiles, kitchenware, books, toys and a large selection of Moomin pieces.

219 MONOLOGUE

93 Redchurch St
E2 7DJ
East ③
+44 (0)20 7729 0400
*www.monologue
london.com*

Another reason to visit new shopping destination Redchurch Street is Monologue. This contemporary concept store sells furniture, lighting, accessories and prints, with a focus on conceptual design from emerging international designers. It's a clean-cut, ever-evolving independent space to discover new and exciting talent.

220 PENTREATH & HALL

17 Rugby St
WC1N 3QT
Bloomsbury ②
+44 (0)20 7430 2526
www.pentreath-hall.com

A small and beautifully arranged shop with a wide range of very English goods and furnishings for the home. The selection reflects the decorative interests of architect Ben Pentreath and designer Bridie Hall, including lighting, glassware, ceramics, stationery, books, wicker baskets and prints by their lodestar artists Eric Ravilious and Edward Bawden.

5 of the most
USEFUL SHOPS

---

221 NOOK

153 Stoke Newington
Church St
N16 0UH
Hackney ⑨
+44 (0)20 7249 9436
www.nookshop.co.uk

Not the biggest shop, but they have certainly found a gap in the market for retailing beautifully well-designed objects that have utility in the home and also work perfectly as gifts. Items for sale include crafted chopping boards, oven gloves, soaps, tea towels, brushes, ceramics and stationery items.

222 LABOUR AND WAIT

85 Redchurch St
E2 7DJ
East ③
+44 (0)20 7729 6253
www.labourandwait.co.uk

One of the first shops to open in the regenerating Redchurch Street, this store sells timeless functional products for everyday life, sourced from specialist makers around the world. Their goods are a range of hardware household items, celebrating simple utility in design.

223 ROMANYS

51 Brewer St
W1F 9UQ
Soho ①
+44 (0)20 7437 4989
www.romanys.co.uk

This ironmongery shop with its historic shopfront has been a fixture in the heart of Soho since 1925. It's packed to the rafters with thousands of densely well-organised products. It is heartening to know that even in rapidly modernising Soho there is still somewhere to buy essentials.

224 **GARDNERS'**

149 Commercial St
E1 6BJ
East ③
+44 (0)20 7247 5119
www.gardnersbags.co.uk

Established in 1870 Gardners' is a fourth generation family business that specialises in supplying paper bags and other sundry items, most frequently to the market traders at the nearby Old Spitalfields Market. The interior is atmospheric and certainly chaotic, with stocks stacked up in steepling piles that teeter in every direction.

225 **LONDON UNDERCOVER**

20 Hanbury St
E1 6QR
East ③
+44 (0)20 7482 4321
www.londonundercover.co.uk

This upmarket little shop, founded in 2008, produces and sells a large range of handcrafted designer umbrellas in modern yet classic fashions. They also sell essential gentleman's accessories and have recently started a small line of outerwear and raincoats. Precise, smart and a celebration of a particularly British style.

221 NOOK

The 5 best places to buy

CONTEMPORARY CRAFTS

226 **CONTEMPORARY APPLIED ARTS**

89 Southwark St
SE1 0HX
Southbank ④
+44 (0)20 7620 0086
www.caa.org.uk

CAA was founded in 1948 to champion and promote the best-applied artists in Britain. Today there are 350 members, elected for their originality and exceptional craft skills. The ground floor is a large gallery space which shows regular solo and themed shows. Downstairs is a shop selling unique functional and decorative pieces at a good range of prices. The applied arts here include jewellery, ceramics, metalwork, textiles, glass, silver and wood.

227 **THE NEW CRAFTSMEN**

34 North Row
W1K 6DG
Mayfair ⑧
+44 (0)20 7148 3190
www.thenewcraftsmen.com

Opened in 2014 and occupying a striking Arts and Crafts building very close to Oxford Street, The New Craftsmen is a showcase for around 75 British artisan craftsmen. Working in textiles, ceramics, glassware, jewellery, silver, furniture, prints and more they create an inspiring selection of pieces including cups, tableware, toys and decorative works.

228 **LONDON GLASSBLOWING**

62-66 Bermondsey St
SE1 3UD
Southbank ④
+44 (0)20 7403 2800
www.londonglassblowing.
co.uk

Founded in 1976, this is one of Britain's foremost glass studios and gallery spaces. From the gallery you can watch the resident artists at work in the studio, making stunning pieces that are unique in their colour, form and structure. Works in the gallery are available for sale, and you can take day classes in glassblowing here too.

229 **FLOW GALLERY**

1-5 Needham Road
W11 2RP
West ⑦
+44 (0)20 7243 0782
www.flowgallery.co.uk

Flow is a commercial gallery in a contemporary space near Westbourne Grove which showcases the work of international artisans and makers from Japan, Scandinavia, Europe and Britain. Throughout the year, they put on special exhibitions of handmade, unusual and unique contemporary crafts. Works include furniture, ceramics, baskets and pieces made with wood, glass, metal and paper.

230 **CONTEMPORARY CERAMICS CENTRE**

63 Great Russell St
WC1B 3BF
Bloomsbury ②
+44 (0)20 7242 9644
www.cpaceramics.com

Directly opposite the British Museum entrance is this ceramics and pottery gallery which exhibits and sells works from members of the Craft Potters Association. There's always an incredibly diverse array of different work and styles on display, showing the best work of contemporary British studios.

The 5 best shops for
ART MATERIALS, PAPER AND PRINTS

---

231 PRESENT & CORRECT

23 Arlington Way
EC1R 1UY
Islington ⑪
+44 (0)20 7278 2460
www.presentandcorrect. com

True heaven for stationery addicts, this smart and beautifully organised modern shop (founded by two graphic designers) stocks a carefully selected range of office essentials, paper products and inspiring ephemera. An old vending machine sells miscellaneous stationery items.

232 L. CORNELISSEN & SON

105A Great Russell St
WC1B 3RY
Clerkenwell ②
+44 (0)20 7636 1045
www.cornelissen.com

This shop near to the British Museum was opened in 1855 and is one of the most beautiful in London with its green exterior and original wooden shelving and storage units. They sell thousands of artists' materials of every kind, many of which are hard to find anywhere else.

233 MATERIAL

124 Evelina Road
SE15 3HL
South ⑤
+44 (0)79 6616 5777
www.materialmaterial.com

This gallery and shop stocks limited edition artists' prints by graphic artists such as Paul Farrell and Heretic, as well as designer stationery and a range of books about graphic art, design and cookery, and children's titles with a strong graphic appeal.

234 MAGMA

29 Shorts Gardens
WC2H 9AP
Covent Garden ①
+44 (0)20 7240 7970
www.magma-shop.com

Magma's smart new concept store is a combination of gallery space, bookshop and designer gift shop. Downstairs is a gallery for print or photo exhibitions and a large selection of creative periodicals. On the ground floor there's a great selection of design, fashion, photography and kids' books and a wide range of prints, gifts and stationery, including their excellent own brand designs.

235 STUART R STEVENSON

68 Clerkenwell Road
EC1M 5QA
Clerkenwell ②
+44 (0)20 7253 1693
www.stuartstevenson.co.uk

This traditional, family-run shop sells a huge selection of artists' supplies and graphic materials. They specialise in gilding materials such as gold and silver leaf, powders and tools for which they have been awarded a royal warrant. In total there are more than 60.000 products stacked floor to ceiling.

234 MAGMA

5 of the best
MARKETS

---

236 BRICK LANE MARKET

Brick Lane
E1 6QR
East ③
www.bricklanemarket.com

The original Brick Lane flea market takes place on Sunday, and sees traders selling a wide range of bric-a-brac, clothing and antiques. Sunday also sees the Upmarket in the Old Truman Brewery area where 140 traders sell crafts, clothes, art, vinyl, bakery and artisan produce.

237 OLD SPITALFIELDS

Horner Square
E1 6EW4
East ③
www.oldspitalfieldsmarket.com

This large covered market in the regenerated Spitalfields area is open every day. Thursday is the antiques market and there's a record fair on the first and third Friday of the month. Saturdays have changing themed markets and on Sundays designers and artists take over.

238 BROADWAY MARKET

Broadway Market
E8 4QJ
Hackney ⑨
www.broadwaymarket.co.uk

Broadway Market has been home to market traders since the 1890s. The street market is a lively, modern affair and takes place on Saturdays with up to 150 stalls selling fresh produce, clothes, art and street food.

239 ALFIE'S ANTIQUE MARKET

13-25 Church St
NW8 8DT
Marylebone ⑧
+44 (0)20 7723 6066
www.alfiesantiques.com

Alfie's is home to dozens of independent traders selling a wide mix of antiques, decorative art and interior design pieces. Various stalls specialise in costume jewellery, clocks, ceramics, glass, porcelain, posters, paintings, 19th- and 20th-century decorative items and much more. It's open Tuesday to Saturday.

240 COLUMBIA ROAD FLOWER MARKET

Columbia Road
E2 7RG
East ③
www.columbiaroad.info

This colourful and lively East End flower market, with its origins in the Victorian era, takes place every Sunday from 8 am till 3 pm. 60 or so independent shops are housed in the distinctive low brick terrace that lines the street selling severally art, crafts, prints, vintage clothes and design items, coffee and refreshments.

237 OLD SPITALFIELDS

BRIXTON RITZY

55 PLACES TO ENJOY CULTURE

———

The 5 best
SMALL GALLERIES

---

241 **DULWICH PICTURE GALLERY**
Gallery Road
SE21 7AD
South ⑤
+44 (0)20 8693 5254
www.dulwichpicture gallery.org.uk

Dulwich opened in 1817 as the world's first purpose-built public gallery. The permanent collection is of Old Master paintings from France, Italy and Spain. Artists represented include Rembrandt, Poussin, Rubens, Canaletto and Gainsborough. They have excellent exhibitions with recent artists including M.C. Escher, Emily Carr and Nikolai Astrup.

242 **WHITECHAPEL GALLERY**
77 Whitechapel High St
E1 7QX
East ③
+44 (0)20 7522 7888
www.whitechapel gallery.org

Founded in 1901 with the aim of bringing art to the people of east London, Whitechapel has a reputation for hosting important exhibitions by international contemporary artists. Recent shows include exhibitions on John Stezaker, Sarah Lucas and Emily Jacir. There's an excellent bookshop run by German booksellers Koenig and a restaurant overseen by Angela Hartnett.

243 WALLACE COLLECTION

Hertford House
Manchester Square
W1U 3BN
Marylebone ⑧
+44 (0)20 7563 9500
www.wallacecollection.org

Grand and historic Hertford House has held the Wallace Collection since 1897. Over 25 galleries display fine and decorative artefacts from the 15th to 19th centuries, with paintings by Titian, Boucher, Van Dyk, Rubens and Velázquez, as well as armour, porcelain, miniatures and furniture. The courtyard has been enclosed with a glass roof and houses a restaurant and cafe.

244 CAMDEN ARTS CENTRE

Arkwright Road
NW3 6DG
North ⑩
+44 (0)20 7472 5500
www.camdenartscentre.org

Founded in 1965 and housed in a former public library, this north London gallery exhibits an innovative and inspiring programme of international contemporary art that often focuses on emerging talents. Recent shows have included Kara Walker and Rose English. There's a bookshop, cafe and garden space too.

245 NEWPORT STREET GALLERY

Newport St
SE11 6AJ
Southbank ④
+44 (0)20 3141 9320
*www.newportstreet
gallery.com*

This exciting new art space opened in 2015 to display selected works from Damien Hirst's art collection, which includes artists as varied as Bacon, Koons, Emin, Banksy and Turk as well as taxidermy and anatomical specimens. The building, a converted warehouse designed by Caruso St John, is elegant with large galleries and high ceilings. Do not exit through the gift shop – it's separate to the galleries, and the only place you'll see Hirst's own works on site.

The 5 best
COMMERCIAL
GALLERIES

---

246 **FINE ARTS SOCIETY**
148 New Bond St
W1S 2JT
Mayfair ⑧
+44 (0)20 7629 5116
www.faslondon.com

The Fine Arts Society was founded in 1876 and its five-storey townhouse now shares space on New Bond Street with the haute couture and jewellery retailers. They specialise in 19th- and 20th-century British art and design, with artists such as Barbara Hepworth, Patrick Heron, Joan Eardley, Samuel Palmer and John Piper. In 2005 they opened the Contemporary Gallery to show modern works.

247 **WHITE CUBE**
144-152 Bermondsey St
SE1 3TQ
Southbank ④
+44 (0)20 7930 5373
www.whitecube.com

This large exhibition space opened in 2011 and is the latest of Jay Joplin's White Cube galleries to open in London. He represents a stellar list of artists including Anselm Kiefer, Tracey Emin, Gilbert and George, Andreas Gursky, Darren Almond and Christian Marclay. There are three large, elegant rooms with polished concrete floors.

248 VICTORIA MIRO
16 Wharf Road
N1 7RW
Islington ⑪
+44 (0)20 7336 8109
www.victoria-miro.com

Victoria Miro has been a London gallerist with a growing reputation since 1985, opening this large space in the Hackney - Islington borders in 2000. The gallery has its own garden and landscaped area overlooking Regent's Canal. Among the artists she represents are Yayoi Kusama, Grayson Perry, Peter Doig and Chris Ofili.

249 LISSON GALLERY
27 Bell St
NW1 5BU
Marylebone ⑧
+44 (0)20 7724 2739
www.lissongallery.com

Lisson is a pioneering and influential gallery with a fine reputation for showing minimal and conceptual artists and sculptors. Opened in 1967 by Nicholas Logsdail, it today represents an exciting roster of artists including Marina Abramovic, Broomberg & Chanarin, Anish Kapoor, Ai Weiwei and Richard Long.

250 GAGOSIAN
6-24 Britannia Street
WC1X 9JD
Bloomsbury ②
+44 (0)20 7841 9960
www.gagosian.com

Larry Gagosian is a US super-dealer of modern art with galleries in cities all across the world. This large exhibition space in London is very close to King's Cross station. Any of the artists he represents, including Takashi Murakami, Rachel Whiteread, Cy Twombly, Howard Hodgkin and Ed Ruscha, might be exhibited.

The 5 best
INDEPENDENT CINEMAS

---

251 BRIXTON RITZY
BRIXTON OVAL
Coldharbour Lane
SW2 1JG
South ⑤
+44 (0)871 902 5739
*www.picturehouses.com/
cinema/Ritzy_Picturehouse*

The Ritzy is the one of the UK's largest independent cinemas with five screens, two bars and a cafe. It was built in 1911 as a grand picture palace. Today it shows a mix of independent films, classics, blockbusters and late night screenings. There's also a live venue called Upstairs for alternative live music and comedy.

252 CLOSE-UP FILM CENTRE
97 Sclater St
E1 6HR
East ③
+44 (0)20 3784 7970
www.closeupfilmcentre.com

This superbly intimate repertory arthouse cinema (just 40 seats) is also an extensive library with 20.000 DVDs and books, specialising in independent, early and world cinema, documentaries and experimental film making. The cosy cafe-bar library room is worth a visit in itself.

253 PRINCE CHARLES CINEMA
7 Leicester Place
WC2H 7BY
Soho ①
+44 (0)20 7494 3654
www.princecharlescinema.com

The Prince Charles is a quirky place that mainly shows repertory, classic, cult, arthouse and genre films. They also stage regular 'sing-a-long-a' performances of films like *The Sound of Music* and *Moulin Rouge*, as well as all-nighter screenings of film series.

254 THE GATE CINEMA

87 Notting Hill Gate
W11 3JZ
West ⑦
+44 (0)871 902 5731
*www.picturehouses.com/
cinema/Gate_Picturehouse*

This arthouse cinema has a small-scale grandeur. The ornate, comfortable and cosy auditorium has elaborate stuccoed ceilings, tables between the seats for drinks and snacks, and sofas at the back. As well as independent films they regularly show live transmissions of opera, ballet and theatre.

255 BFI SOUTHBANK

Belvedere Road
SE1 8XT
Southbank ④
+44 (0)20 7928 3232
www.whatson.bfi.org.uk

The British Film Institute occupies a wonderful position on the Southbank underneath Waterloo Bridge. The four screens are programmed with regular seasons of classic, independent and foreign films and frequent director retrospectives and genre-themed festivals. The cinema has two bars and an excellent shop selling books on cinema and DVDs.

251 BRIXTON RITZY

The 5 most
INNOVATIVE THEATRES

256 ARCOLA THEATRE
24 Ashwin St
E8 3DL
Hackney ⑨
+44 (0)20 7503 1646
www.arcolatheatre.com

Arcola is a locally engaged and internationally minded theatre that has a growing reputation under the artistic directorship of Mehmet Ergen. There's an exciting and diverse programme of challenging plays by new writers, as well as opera and musicals. It's a boutique-sized theatre but it has great ambition, showcasing cutting-edge work from emerging companies.

257 BUSH THEATRE
7 Uxbridge Road
W12 8LJ
West ⑦
+44 (0)20 8743 5050
www.bushtheatre.co.uk

This small, good-value and friendly theatre has long had an international reputation as a home for new plays and exciting voices. Recently moved into a former community library next to Shepherd's Bush Market, it has 144 seats, a garden space and cafe bar. Their provocative and entertaining programme commissions work from leading and emerging companies across the world.

258 **ROYAL COURT THEATRE**
Sloane Square
SW1W 8AS
South West ⑥
+44 (0)20 7565 5000
www.royalcourttheatre.
com

The Royal Court has had an international reputation since opening in 1956, and is still at the forefront of creating restless and provocative theatre about contemporary issues. The English Stage Company is resident, performing the work of new and international writers. The 19th-century red-brick building is grand and Italianate, housing a small downstairs and large upstairs theatre, and a cafe bar.

259 **YOUNG VIC**
66 The Cut
SE1 8LZ
Southbank ④
+44 (0)20 7922 2922
www.youngvic.org

The Young Vic is known for being a 'directors' theatre' with David Lan programming eclectic and leftfield productions of new and classic plays and attracting directors from around the world. In recent years its reputation has only increased for staging progressive and innovate productions. As well as the light-industrial and intimate Main House there are two studio spaces and a good bar kitchen.

260 **THE YARD**
Unit 2a
Queen's Yard
White Post Lane
E9 5EN
Hackney ⑨
+44 (0)7548 156 266
www.theyardtheatre.co.uk

This new and exciting fringe theatre, located in the warehouse hinterlands near the Olympic Park, performs award-winning work by new writers. The venue seats 111 and is a converted courtyard warehouse with corrugated roof and concrete floor. It has a growing reputation for putting on late-night DJ events at weekends.

The 5 most inspiring
CULTURAL CENTRES

---

261 **INSTITUTE FOR CONTEMPORARY ARTS**
The Mall
SW1Y 5AH
Mayfair ⑧
+44 (0)20 7930 3647
www.ica.org.uk

The ICA is a multi-disciplinary venue that has been promoting radical art and culture since it opened in 1946. There are exhibitions of conceptual and modern art (including the annual Bloomberg New Contemporaries show), two cinemas showing arthouse and experimental filmmaking, cutting edge live music and DJ performances, as well as talks and discussions.

262 **RICH MIX**
35-47 Bethnal Green Road
E1 6LA
East ③
+44 (0)20 7613 7498
www.richmix.org.uk

Housed in a former leather factory between Shoreditch and Bethnal Green, Rich Mix promotes a broad range of multicultural artistic activities. There are three cinemas showing arthouse and blockbuster films and multiple flexible performance spaces that stage theatre, talks, art exhibitions, comedy and a wide and eclectic range of music from around the world.

263 BARBICAN CENTRE

Silk St
EC2Y 8DS
Clerkenwell ②
+44 (0)20 7638 8891
www.barbican.org.uk

The Barbican building is a Brutalist architectural icon in itself. Its arts centre is one of the best venues for classical music and stages exciting contemporary, jazz and world concerts too. There's also a theatre, cinema complex and a large art exhibition space, as well as restaurants, shops and cafes. Architectural tours are available and the secluded outside courtyard space by the lake is magical.

264 BRITISH LIBRARY

96 Euston Road
NW1 2DB
Bloomsbury ②
+44 (0)20 7412 7332
www.bl.uk

The national library is under-rated as a cultural venue. The Treasures Gallery houses wonders including the Magna Carta, Gutenberg's bible, Beatles lyrics and Leonardo da Vinci manuscripts. Special exhibitions have featured subjects as diverse as punk music, cartography, comics and Lewis Carroll. They run a busy programme of events, concerts, discussions, and classes.

265 SOUTHBANK CENTRE

Belvedere Road
SE1 8XX
Southbank ④
+44 (0)20 7960 4200
www.southbankcentre. co.uk

In an enviable position on the river the Southbank Centre is a multi-venue cultural hotspot with an all-encompassing and accessible programme. Contemporary international art is exhibited in the Hayward Gallery whilst the Royal Festival and Queen Elizabeth Halls stage a wide range of classical and contemporary music.

5 artworks to see at
TATE BRITAIN

Tate Britain
Millbank
SW1P 4RG
South West ⑥
+44 (0)20 7887 8888
www.tate.org.uk/visit/tate-britain

266 **LANDSCAPE AT IDEN**
PAUL NASH
1929

War artist Paul Nash (1889-1946) played a key role in the development of modernism in Britain, and is one of the most important painters of the 20th century. This symbolic landscape painting has an uncanny feel with its dramatic perspectives and seemingly unrelated objects, showing the influence of surrealism.

267 **1935 (WHITE RELIEF)**
BEN NICHOLSON
1935

Ben Nicholson (1894-1982) was influenced by the emerging avant-garde movement and by the British sculptors Hepworth and Moore, to become an abstract painter with a distinctive style of his own. This monochrome relief sculpture of white paint on wood contains the clean and sharply defined lines of right angles and circles.

268 LATE MORNING
BRIDGET RILEY
1967-1968

One of the foremost exponents of Op-art, Bridget Riley's (°1931) early works were predominantly only black and white. *Late Morning* is one of her first experiments with using colour.
The vertical stripes in this large painting act as a neural structure in which the rhythms of carefully chosen colour variations bring the painting alive.

269 RED SLATE CIRCLE
RICHARD LONG
1988

Richard Long (°1945) is one of the best known practitioners of Land Art. His works are created by walking in the natural environment and explore the relationship between man and nature. Some pieces are temporary and created in situ, others created with photography and text after the event. This sculpture, formed of a circle of jagged textured rocks, is an example of his gallery work that incorporates found objects.

270 THE HISTORY OF THE WORLD
JEREMY DELLER
1997-2004

Jeremy Deller (°1966) is a conceptual artist whose works often involve collaborations. This diagram explores the social, political and musical connections between house music and brass bands in Britain, and provided the conceptual backbone for his Acid Brass project. This involved a traditional brass band playing acid house classics.

5 things to see at the
V&A MUSEUM

Victoria and Albert Museum
Cromwell Road
SW7 2RL
South West ⑥
+44 (0)20 7942 2000
www.vam.ac.uk

271 **TIPU'S TIGER**
ROOM 41

This extraordinary late 18th-century work depicts an awesome life-sized Indian tiger made of carved and painted wood that's in the process of devouring a prostrate colonialist. Concealed inside the body is a mechanical wind-up organ. The work was made for Tipu, Sultan of Mysore.

272 **FURNITURE GALLERY**
ROOMS 133-5

Of course you must visit the fashion, jewellery, Asian and sculpture galleries, but don't miss the furniture collection on level 6. Telling the story of the design and production of furniture over the last 600 years and including over 200 pieces, it features pieces by Thomas Chippendale, Frank Lloyd Wright, Eileen Grey, Charles and Ray Eames, Tom Dixon and Ron Arad.

273 LYDIA DWIGHT DEAD
ROOM 58C

Created in 1674, this remarkable portrait sculpture of a dead girl of six years of age lying on a pillow is a highly personal and moving memorial to a daughter. It was produced by John Dwight at the Fulham Pottery and is a very beautiful work that was intended to be private and to perpetuate her memory.

274 NORFOLK HOUSE MUSIC ROOM
ROOM 52

Norfolk House was built in 1722 in St James' Square. It was one of the first grand houses to have a room dedicated to the performance of music, which was designed by Giovanni Battista Borra. The house was demolished in 1938 but the interiors were saved and restored. The panelled walls, doorways, mirrors and ceilings are on display here. The room is used for free evening concerts.

275 MORRIS, GAMBLE AND POYNTER ROOMS

The V&A was the first museum in the world to have restaurant and refreshment rooms – they were built in the 1860s and 70s and are still the most spectacular. Conceived as an opportunity to showcase modern design and craftsmanship, leading designers of the day including William Morris were commissioned to decorate the stunning rooms.

The 5 best sound systems at
NOTTING HILL CARNIVAL

---

276 ABA SHANTI-I
Corner of East Row and
West Row

Aba Shanti has been holding down a spot at Carnival since 1993, and before that his Antiguan father ran a sound system called Count Alan. They play roots music, dub and reggae with added reverb, delays and effects to create a heady and uplifting mix. Expect heavy dubplate rhythms with conscious lyrics and spiritual vibes.

277 GAZ'S ROCKIN' BLUES
159 Wardour Street
www.gazrockin.com

Gaz Mayall, son of the legendary Bluesbreaker John Mayall, has been DJing at Carnival since 1982 and has been running Gaz's Rockin' Blues at this location since the late 80s. An elaborate and themed stage is built each year and features a number of energetic DJs and live bands playing ska, reggae, revival, New Orleans R&B and rock'n'roll.

278 **CHANNEL ONE**

Leamington Road Villas
Westbourne Park Road
*www.channelone
soundsystem.com*

This internationally renowned sound system is run by Mikey Dread and his brother Jah T. Playing new and old dub and reggae on a single deck with echo, sirens and MCs riding over the top, their music spreads a positive message of unity and strength through Rastafari. Their huge and elaborate speaker stack designs are custom built.

279 **RAPATTACK**

23 All Saints Road
+44 (0)786 058 0582
www.rapattack.co.uk

Since the unfortunate demise of Norman Jay's Good Times sound system Rapattack has been the best bet at Carnival for finding a good mix of party tunes from the 1970s to the present. Playing funk, soul, hip-hop, R&B, disco, UK and US garage and house, they've been a fixture at Notting Hill since 1984.

280 **RAMPAGE**

Colville Road
www.rampagesound.com

This huge sound system attracts a big crowd at what is one of the larger spots at Carnival near Colville Gardens. DJ Mike Anthony and crew play an upfront mix of urban styles including R&B, bashment, hip-hop, and UK Garage. They often attract some big name live acts and singers to perform on their stage.

The 5 best venues for
LIVE MUSIC

---

281 CAFE OTO
18-22 Ashwin St
E8 3DL
Hackney ⑨
+44 (0)20 7923 1231
www.cafeoto.co.uk

Undoubtedly one of the most exciting venues with an amazing experimental music programme. It's an intimate space with low ceilings, brick walls and no raised stage. Local and international acts perform free jazz, avant-garde, psych rock, folk, noise, improv, electronics and world music. By day there's an excellent cafe kitchen serving Persian food and great cakes. There's also a small record shop.

282 THE VORTEX
11 Gillett Square
N16 8AZ
Hackney ⑨
+44 (0)20 7254 4097
www.vortexjazz.co.uk

This community-minded and non-profit little jazz venue is one of the best jazz spots in the country. The diverse and innovative programming nurtures new talent and features jazz in its many varied guises including contemporary, improv, free, fusion and gypsy. There's a bar cafe downstairs in addition to the small upstairs main room.

283 MOTH CLUB

Old Trades Hall
Valette St
E9 6NU
Hackney ⑨
+44 (0)20 8985 7963
www.mothclub.co.uk

The Memorable Order of Tin Hats is a bizarre and exciting new venue housed within the confines of a still functioning military veterans club. The glittery update of the traditional interior is magical. Entertainments vary from the latest avant-indie and pop to themed quiz nights, bingo and film screenings.

284 WILTON'S MUSIC HALL

1 Graces Alley
E1 8JB
East ③
+44 (0)20 7702 2789
www.wiltons.org.uk

Tucked away behind a row of terraced houses this historic East End music hall dates from 1859 and is the oldest surviving example of its type. It has recently been refurbished, but with care not to diminish the wonderful atmosphere and sense of age. They put on a distinctive range of concerts and events including opera, piano sonatas, musical theatre, swing dance, cabaret and magic.

285 KING'S PLACE

90 York Way
N1 9AG
Islington ⑪
+44 (0)20 7520 1490
www.kingsplace.co.uk

Located in the redeveloped King's Cross area and sharing a building with The Guardian newspaper, this venue has a modern, purpose-built concert hall with amazing acoustics and a stunning oak veneer décor. The hall is moderately sized with the programming weighted towards chamber and classical music but also including world, folk, jazz, choral and poetry.

The 5 best
MUSIC FESTIVALS

---

286 LONDON JAZZ FESTIVAL
VARIOUS VENUES
www.efglondon
jazzfestival.org.uk

Taking place every November over ten days the London Jazz Festival represents a huge range of styles from mainstream to experimental, and gigs can take place in the largest concert halls or smallest jazz clubs. In all around 2000 artists are involved each year in more than 300 concerts across 50 different venues. It's one of the top jazz festivals in the world.

287 FIELD DAY
VICTORIA PARK
Grove Road
E3 5TB
Hackney ⑨
www.fielddayfestivals.com

Taking place in early June since 2007, Field Day has been programming interesting, innovative and on-trend line-ups that join the indie, club and hipster tribes. It takes place across a number of stages in Victoria Park, including the new hangar-like indoor dance arena The Barn. The Village Mentality area recreates the frivolity of a country summer fayre.

288 **MELTDOWN**
SOUTHBANK CENTRE
Belvedere Road
SE1 8XX
Southbank ④
+44 (0)20 7960 4200

Each year the Southbank Centre invites a luminary of the music world to be guest director of its week-long Meltdown festival. Previous curators have included David Byrne, Jarvis Cocker, Lee 'Scratch' Perry, Patti Smith, Massive Attack and Yoko Ono. They invite their favourite artists to perform special shows and initiate collaborations and one-off performances.

289 **TRANSCENDER**
BARBICAN CENTRE
Silk St
EC2Y 8DS
Clerkenwell ②
+44 (0)20 7638 8891
www.barbican.org.uk/
transcender

Focusing on music designed to transport the listener and conjure trances, the Barbican's innovative week-long Transcender festival is a mix of traditional and contemporary styles that may include cosmic jazz, psych rock, minimalism and international sacred music. It takes place every autumn and combines special commissions and unusual collaborations.

290 **LOVEBOX**
VICTORIA PARK
Tower Hamlets
E3 5TB
Hackney ⑨
www.loveboxfestival.com

Lovebox was founded in 2003 by the DJ duo Groove Armada, aiming to recreate the hedonistic country festival vibe in the city. It takes place over two days with many stages and tents playing host to a huge range of big-name and upcoming soul, funk, hip-hop, R&B and reggae live acts, plus underground DJs playing contemporary dance and electronic styles.

5 historic
CHURCHES for
LIVE MUSIC

---

291 **ST JOHN AT HACKNEY**
Lower Clapton Road
E5 0PD
Hackney ⑨
+44 (0)20 8985 5374

This working church, built in 1792, is one of London's most unique spaces for music. The classical architecture, high ceilings and natural light create an atmosphere that is at once epic and intimate. St John Sessions run an irregular programme of alternative and experimental music here, featuring diverse and exciting artists.

292 **UNION CHAPEL**
19B Compton Terrace
N1 2UN
Islington ⑪
+44 (0)20 7226 1686
www.unionchapel.org.uk

Built in the grand Gothic Revival style in the late 19th century, this working Grade I listed church has been host to many unique and special candlelit concerts. Music featured has included folk, indie, pop, jazz, world and even the laid-back sounds of the Big Chill club, with artists such as Bjork, Youssou N'Dour and Philip Glass.

293 ST MARTIN IN THE FIELD

Trafalgar Square
WC2N 4JJ
Covent Garden ①
+44 (0)20 7766 1100
*www.stmartin-in-the-fields.
org/music*

This Georgian Neoclassical church was built in 1726 and enjoys a prominent position on Trafalgar Square. As well as being a fully active church it hosts a huge programme of musical concerts. Sacred, choral, chamber, baroque and early-classical music is played in the church, with weekly jazz concerts taking place in the Cafe in the Crypt below ground.

294 LSO ST LUKE'S

161 Old St
EC1V 9NG
East ③
+44 (0)20 7638 8891
www.lso.co.uk/lso-st-lukes

Built in 1733, this Grade I listed Hawksmoor church, with its unusual obelisk spire, lay ruined for 40 years before being restored to become a home to the London Symphony Orchestra. A diverse range of music events are performed here including choral works, small classical groups, LSO rehearsals and regular free lunchtime concerts.

295 ROUND CHAPEL

Clapton Park URC
Powerscroft Road
E5 0PU
Hackney ⑨
+44 (0)20 8533 9676
*www.theroundchapel.
org.uk*

This unusual nonconformist church was built in 1871 and is remarkable for its near-round shape, iron pillars and encircling balcony. As well as being an active church the building is used for community and arts projects, including events such as beer festivals and vintage fairs. It's also used for contemporary music concerts and even club events.

FOURNIER STREET

50 PLACES TO DISCOVER HISTORIC LONDON

5 *secret*
HISTORIC STREETS

296 **FOURNIER STREET**
  E1 6QE
  East ③

This street is one of the most important and best-preserved examples of early Georgian townhouses in Britain. First settled by French Huguenots in the 1720s the area has subsequently been populated by Jewish and Bengali communities and today is home to artists Gilbert and George and Tracey Emin.

297 **ARNOLD CIRCUS**
  E2 7JS
  East ③

Arnold Circus and the Boundary Estate's radiating multi-storey brick tenements can be considered the world's first council housing, completed in 1900. The area was an impoverished East End slum; the mound in the middle of the circus, where a bandstand is still extant, was created from materials demolished by the clearance.

298 **CECIL COURT**
  WC2N 4EZ
  Covent Garden ①

This atmospheric pedestrianised alley off Charing Cross Road dates to the end of the 17th century, and is today home to around 20 antiquarian and specialist booksellers. The street was named after Robert Cecil, the 1st Earl of Salisbury.

299 ROUPELL STREET

SE1 8SP
Southbank ④

This street of Georgian worker's cottages is incredibly well-preserved. The small, dark-bricked terraced properties were built by developer and landlord John Roupell in 1824. Today the street is often used for period film and television sets. The Kings Arms pub dates from the same time and is worth a visit.

300 CABLE STREET

E1 0AE
East ③

This street got its name from the ship ropes which were made from cables laid along the street in this dockland area. In 1936 it was the scene of The Battle of Cable Street: an infamous confrontation that occurred when a group of anti-fascists rallied and forced back a march by Oswald Mosley's blackshirted British Union of Fascists. A mural on St George's Town Hall depicts the events.

296 FOURNIER STREET

297 ARNOLD CIRCUS

5 of the most
CURIOUS BUILDINGS

---

301 BRITAIN'S SMALLEST POLICE STATION

Trafalgar Square
WC2N 5BY
Covent Garden ①

This unassuming building in the south-east corner of Trafalgar Square was designed as a hidden place for police to observe public demonstrations. Resembling a stone pillar it features discreet black doors with small paned windows and has an ornamental iron light fitting on top. It was built in 1926 and fitted with a direct phone line to Scotland Yard. No longer in use, it would have accommodated two officers at a squeeze.

302 LONDON SILVER VAULTS

Chancery House
53-64 Chancery Lane
WC2A 1QS
Clerkenwell ②
+44 (0)20 7242 3844
www.silvervaultslondon.com

Built in 1876 these were underground strong rooms with walls 1.2 metres thick and lined with steel, to be rented out to hold valuables for the public. Over time it became used by silver dealers and is today home to around 40 shops selling silver to the public. Each one is located in a rather cramped underground cell and has never been broken into.

303 THE MONUMENT

Fish St Hill/Monument St
EC3R 8AH
City ④
www.themonument.info

This Doric column, topped with a gilded urn of fire, was completed in 1677 as a Monument to the 1666 Great Fire of London. Its 62-metre height is equal to the distance from where it stands to the origin of the fire, a bakery in Pudding Lane. The Monument is open to the public and visitors can climb the 311 steps to get a great panoramic view.

304 EXECUTION DOCK

Wapping Old Stairs
62 Wapping High St
E1W 2PN
East ③
www.the-east-end.co.uk/
execution-dock

The exact location of Execution Dock is unclear but it is likely to have been near the Wapping Old Stairs, which are accessed from a narrow passageway by the Town of Ramsgate pub. A large scaffold for hanging was erected in the river below the low-tide line for the execution of pirates, smugglers and mutineers. It was used for more than 400 years until around 1830.

305 VIADUCT TAVERN

126 Newgate Street
EC1A 7AA
City ④
www.viaducttavern.co.uk

This historic pub was named after the nearby Holborn Viaduct. Built on the site of a former jail, the cellar is said to contain five former cells. These are visible to the public. The pub has a fine interior and is notable for having a rare 'toll booth' at the bar, from where the landlord would sell beer tokens in order to keep cash out of the bar workers' hands.

5 places to understand
LONDON'S HISTORY

---

306 LONDON WALL
LONDON WALL (ROAD) - WEST
EC2Y 5HN
City ④

The London Wall was built by the Romans between AD 190 and 225. Outside the Museum of London there are some visible remains of the wall that once encircled the old City.

307 ELECTRIC AVENUE
SW9 8JP
South ⑤

This street in Brixton was built in the 1880s and was among the first in Britain to be lit by electricity. Today it's partly the location of the Brixton food market. In 1983 it was the subject for an electro-reggae hit by Eddy Grant.

308 BREWER STREET CAR PARK
Brewer Street
W1F 0LA
Soho ①
www.brewerstreetcarpark.com

This wonderful art-deco car park, built in 1929 and still in use today, is one of the earliest examples of a ramped multi-storey car park. During the 1950s and 60s it was apparently a location for shady payoffs to the police from the local red-light industry. More recently the car park has hosted the London Fashion Week, and has been used for art installations.

309 PUDDING LANE

EC3R 8AB
City ④

This small and unremarkable-looking street was where the devastating Great Fire of London of 1666 started inside Thomas Farriner's bakery. It quickly spread, raging for two days and gutting most of medieval London including St Paul's Cathedral. Today a plaque marks the spot where the bakery stood. The street is said to be named after the offal (pudding) that fell off butcher's carts into the lane.

310 ST JOHN'S GATE

St John's Lane
EC1M 4BU
Clerkenwell ②

This impressive brick and stone gate was built in 1504 as the entrance to the Priory of the Knights of St John, one of few remnants of London's monastic past. In the early 18th century painter William Hogarth lived here. Today it houses the Museum of the Order of St John.

308 BREWER STREET CAR PARK

5

FASCINATING CEMETERIES

311 **BUNHILL FIELDS**
38 City Road
EC1Y 1AU
East ③

This atmospheric old burial nonconformist ground near Old Street station is nowadays open as a public garden. It is the burial site of John Bunyan (*Paradise Lost*), Daniel Defoe (*Robinson Crusoe*), the artist, poet and visionary William Blake and Susanna Wesley ('Mother of Methodism') amongst others.

312 **CROSS BONES BURIAL GROUND**
Redcross Way
SE1 1TA
Southbank ④

Borough's burial ground for the 'outcast dead' holds an estimated 15.000 bodies buried on top of one other in unmarked graves. The unconsecrated graveyard was closed in 1853, and is thought likely to have been used for paupers, criminals and prostitutes. Today there's a pretty memorial garden and shrine on the site.

313 **OLD ST PANCRAS CHURCHYARD**
Pancras Road
NW1 1UL
North ⑩
www.posp.co.uk/ old-st-pancras

Old St Pancras Church dates back to the 4th century. It's the site of a number of significant burials including writer and philosopher Mary Wollstonecraft and her husband William Godwin, architect John Soane and composer Johann Christian Bach.

314 HIGHGATE CEMETERY

Swain's Lane
N6 6PJ
North ⑲
+44 (0)20 8340 1834
www.highgatecemetery.org

With its many Victorian mausoleums and tombstones and a wonderful range of plants and wildlife, this is one of the most beautiful cemeteries. Just a few of the famous people buried here are Karl Marx, Radclyffe Hall, Patrick Caulfield and Douglas Adams.

315 ABNEY PARK CEMETERY

Stoke Newington High St
N16 0LH
Hackney ⑨
+44 (0)20 7275 7557
www.abneypark.org

This cemetery lies in a large historic parkland area with an arboretum. There are a number of notable Victorian nonconformist burials here including the founders of the Salvation Army William and Catherine Booth, anti-slavery campaigners and theatre and music hall stars.

311 BUNHILL FIELDS

The 5 best
SMALL MUSEUMS

316 GEFFRYE MUSEUM

136 Kingsland Road
E2 8EA
East ③
+44 (0)20 7739 9893
*www.geffrye-museum.
org.uk*

The Geffrye offers a fascinating glimpse into how normal lives have been lived over the last 400 years. The museum, with 11 chronologically presented period rooms, is housed in historic brick almshouse buildings dating from 1714. There are also special exhibitions and period gardens to see.

317 FASHION AND TEXTILE MUSEUM

83 Bermondsey St
SE1 3XF
Southbank ④
+44 (0)20 7407 8664
www.ftmlondon.org

One of the first enterprises to locate in regenerating Bermondsey Street, the Fashion and Textile Museum opened in 2003. It was founded by textile designer Zandra Rhodes. It presents a series of innovative special exhibitions focusing on textiles, clothing, jewellery, brands and fashion history in 20th- and 21st-century Britain.

318 HUNTERIAN MUSEUM

Royal College of
Surgeons
35 Lincoln's Inn Fields
WC2A 3PE
City ④
+44 (0)20 7869 6560
www.hunterianmuseum.org

The Hunterian shows the amazing collection of human and non-human anatomical specimens, surgical instruments and art relating to surgical science that was originally John Hunter's, an 18th-century surgeon and anatomist. It celebrates the historic advances in science, and is a fascinating and occasionally gruesome spectacle.

319 CARTOON MUSEUM

35 Little Russell St
WC1A 2HH
Bloomsbury ②
+44 (0)20 7580 8155
www.cartoonmuseum.org

This modest but excellent collection celebrates the rich heritage of British cartoons, political caricatures, comic strips and animation from the 18th century to the present day, with original pieces ranging from strips for children's comic The Beano to satirical works by James Gillray.

320 GRANT MUSEUM OF ZOOLOGY

Rockefeller Building
21 University Street
WC1E 6DE
Bloomsbury ②
+44 (0)20 3108 2052
www.ucl.ac.uk/museums/ zoology

Stuffed with 68.000 specimens in avenues of display cases this brilliant natural history museum is housed in a former library at University College in Bloomsbury. It was established in 1828 and has evolved since then into a fine museum that includes myriad zoological specimens, taxidermy, jars of preserved animals, dodo bones, bisected heads and a quagga skeleton.

The 5 most
UNUSUAL MUSEUMS

321 MUSEUM OF BRANDS, PACKAGING AND ADVERTISING

111-117 Lancaster Road
W11 1QT
West ⑦
+44 (0)20 7243 9611
www.museumofbrands.com

A huge collection of domestic and everyday products and packaging of food and household items, posters, toys, games and printed media. Chronologically organised, from the Victorian period to the present day, this nostalgic and engrossing treasure trove details the history of consumer culture.

322 WELLCOME COLLECTION

183 Euston Road
NW1 2BE
Bloomsbury ②
+44 (0)20 7611 2222
www.wellcomecollection. org

Billing itself as a museum for the "incurably curious" the Wellcome displays a highly unusual mixture of medical artefacts and original artworks that explore the connections between medicine, life and art. Based on the huge and varied collections of Sir Henry Wellcome, the permanent displays are fascinating and occasionally macabre. The innovative and exciting special exhibitions have included shows on the subjects of death, the brain, sex and dirt.

323 VIKTOR WYND MUSEUM OF CURIOSITIES

11 Mare St
E8 4RP
Hackney ⑨
+44 (0)20 7998 3617
www.thelasttuesdaysociety.org/museum-curiosities

Beneath The Last Tuesday Society's cocktail bar and literary salon lies Viktor Wynd's collection of curiosities, fine art and natural history: a fascinating, bizarre and often grotesque assortment of objects that evoke the pre-enlightenment origins of museums. Butterflies, two-headed kittens and lambs, taxidermy, tribal art and occultist pieces are all on display, and much more besides.

324 KIRKALDY TESTING MUSEUM

99 Southwark St
SE1 0JF
Southbank ④
+44 (0)20 7998 3617
www.testingmuseum.org.uk

This very unusual museum houses the 47 foot long, 116 tonne Kirkaldy Testing Machine, able to exert a million pounds of pressure and to determine the tensile strength of any object. The museum is housed in 19th-century engineer David Kirkaldy's original testing works. Only open on the first Sunday of the month.

325 OLD OPERATING MUSEUM AND HERB GARRET

9A St Thomas St
SE1 9RY
Southbank ④
+44 (0)20 7188 2679
www.thegarret.org.uk

This unique museum houses the oldest surviving operating theatre in Britain, dating from 1822 – the age before anaesthetics and antiseptics. A collection of artefacts relating to the horror of medicine before the advance of science is on display. The site was also an herb apothecary where natural remedies, including opium, were grown for the hospital.

5 of the most
REMARKABLE
CHURCHES

---

326 ST DUNSTAN IN THE EAST
Dunstan's Hill
EC3R 5DD
City ④

This ruined City church is now the site of a beautifully secluded and peaceful garden, hidden away below towering office buildings. It was originally built around 1100 and was badly damaged in the Great Fire of London, before being rebuilt with a tower and spire designed by Sir Christopher Wren. The church again suffered damage during the Blitz. Only the tower, spire and north and south walls remain today. It's an uncanny and evocative place.

327 CHRIST CHURCH, SPITALFIELDS
Commercial St
E1 6LY
East ③
+44 (0)20 7377 2440
*www.christchurch
spitalfields.org*

Renowned church architect Nicholas Hawksmoor's English Baroque masterpiece (built 1714-19) is hugely impressive, towering over the Spitalfields area with its angular and unique Portland stone façade. The exterior, interior and the famous organ have all been recently restored. One of London's most singular buildings.

328 TEMPLE CHURCH

Temple
EC4Y 7BB
City ④
+44 (0)20 7353 3470
www.templechurch.com

This unique 12th-century church stands amongst the courtyards, greenery and ancient buildings of Temple's peaceful Inns of Court, home to ancient societies of lawyers. It has an unusual round design and remarkable stone effigies of a number of the Knights Templar, the secretive order of crusading monks who built it. Services, choral concerts and organ recitals are held here.

329 ST OLAVE'S CHURCH

8 Hart St
EC3R 7NB
City ④
+44 (0)20 7488 4318

St Olave's is a modest building in the Perpendicular Gothic style, with the feel of a rural parish church hidden away in the City. The entrance is decorated with macabre grimacing skulls, leading Charles Dickens to immortalise it as 'St Ghastly the Grim' in one of his novels.

330 ST STEPHEN'S CHURCH WALBROOK

39 Walbrook
EC4N 8BN
City ④
+44 (0)20 7626 9000
www.ststephenwalbrook. net

Built 1672-9, this magnificent church was designed by Sir Christopher Wren. Behind an unassuming exterior hides one of his very finest interiors, featuring a domed roof design that was later used for St Paul's. Critic Nikolaus Pevsner rated it as one of the ten most important English buildings. The circular modern altar is by Henry Moore.

331 **YE OLDE CHESHIRE CHEESE**
145 Fleet St
EC4A 2BU
City ④
+44 (0)20 7353 6170

This characterful pub dates back to 1538. It has numerous bars and a dozen rooms split over four levels. The dark wood-panelled walls and low lighting have attracted many literary drinkers over the years, including Dickens, Wodehouse, Chesterton, Tennyson and Conan Doyle. Look out for the remains of Polly the Parrot who held court here for 40 years.

332 **THE MAYFLOWER**
117 Rotherhithe St
SE16 4NF
Southbank ④
+44 (0)20 7237 4088
www.mayflowerpub.co.uk

The Mayflower was the boat chartered by the Pilgrim Fathers to sail across the Atlantic in 1620. The boat was moored outside this 16th-century Rotherhithe pub before it set sail to the New World. The pub is incredibly atmospheric and cosy with an open fire and wooden pews.

333 **SEVEN STARS**
53-54 Carey St
WC2A 2JB
City ④
+44 (0)20 7242 8521

This cosy, charming and slightly eccentric pub, dating from 1602, is located on a quiet, tucked-away street behind the buildings of the Royal Courts of Justice. There are curious window displays and a pleasing interior that reflect the legal associations of the pub.

334 CITTIE OF YORKE

22 High Holborn
WC1V 6BN
Clerkenwell ②
+44 (0)20 7242 7670

There has been a pub on this site since around 1430, and although the current interiors date from the early 20th century they have a strong medieval feel to them. The enormous main hall with its long wooden bar, high beams and cosy wooden booths has a baronial grandeur.

335 YE OLDE MITRE

1 Ely Court
EC1N 6SJ
Clerkenwell ②
+44 (0)20 7405 4751
www.yeoldemitreholborn. co.uk

The Mitre is probably the most secret pub in London. It dates from 1546 and the present building from 1773. There's a small outdoor courtyard area and inside it's a cosy and welcoming traditional pub. Due to a strange ecclesiastical anomaly it is considered to be a part of Cambridgeshire.

333 SEVEN STARS

5 *fascinating*
HOMES OPEN
TO THE PUBLIC

336 **SIR JOHN SOANE'S MUSEUM**
13 Lincoln's Inn Fields
WC2A 3BP
City ④
+44 (0)20 7405 2107
www.soane.org

Sir John Soane (1753-1837) was an English Neoclassical architect. His house has been untouched since his death and is full of curiosities and surprises. The adapted interiors and their use of natural light ingeniously showcase this world class collection of artworks, sculptures, antiquities, furniture and architectural drawings and models.

337 **LEIGHTON HOUSE MUSEUM**
12 Holland Park Road
W14 8LZ
West ⑦
+44 (0) 20 7602 3316
www.rbkc.gov.uk/subsites/ museums

Sir Frederick Leighton (1830-1896) was a painter and Royal Academician. His house contains remarkably elaborate orientalist and aesthetic interiors, including a two-storey 'Arab Hall' decorated with tiles collected in the Middle East and a top-lit upper gallery. As well as many of Leighton's paintings there are works by the Pre-Raphaelite artists Millais, Burne-Jones and Watts.

338 FREUD MUSEUM

20 Maresfield Gardens
NW3 5SX
North ⑩
+44 (0)20 7435 2002
www.freud.org.uk

The Austrian neurologist and father of psychoanalysis Sigmund Freud (1856-1939) lived in this Hampstead house at the end of his life. It contains his psychoanalytic couch as well as a library, furniture, artworks, antiquities and other effects that came with him from Vienna. Exhibitions explain Freud's life and work.

339 DR JOHNSON'S HOUSE

17 Gough Square
EC4A 3DE
City ④
+44 (0)20 7353 3745
www.drjohnsonshouse.org

Dr Samuel Johnson (1709-1784) was an essayist, poet, critic, biographer and, most famously, the author of *A Dictionary of the English Language*, which took nine years to complete. His house, cosseted away in a warren of narrow City streets, is a tranquil place and a fine example of a Georgian interior. It seems apt here to offer one of his most famous quotes: "When a man is tired of London, he is tired of life."

340 DENNIS SEVERS' HOUSE

18 Folgate Street
E1 6BX
East ③
+44 (0)20 7247 4013
www.dennissevershouse. co.uk

This Georgian terraced house in Spitalfields is a totally unique time capsule. It presents a 'still-life drama' told through the portrayal of ten period rooms which recreate the lives of a family of immigrant Huguenot silk-weavers between the years 1724 and 1914. It's a special and evocative place, complete with candlelight and smells – the creation of Denis Severs, an American who lived here until his death in 1999.

5 *notable*

MODERNIST BUILDINGS

341 ISOKON BUILDING
The Isokon Gallery
Lawn Road
NW3 2XD
North ⑲
www.isokongallery.co.uk

This daringly modern, sleek and white-painted concrete apartment building was designed by Wells Coates and completed in 1934. It was a significant experiment in new ways of urban living and became the epicentre of the London avant-garde, with early residents including Walter Gropius and László Moholy-Nagy. Now a gallery has opened there to tell the history of the building and the Modern movement.

342 THE FINNISH CHURCH
33 Albion St
SE16 7JG
Southbank ④
+44 (0)20 7237 1261
www.finnishchurch.org.uk

This Lutheran church in Rotherhithe was built in 1958 as a religious and cultural meeting place for British Finns. The building, designed by Cyrill Mardall-Sjöström, is Grade II listed and has a distinctive storied tower and a main building that incorporates a beautiful church hall. It's a welcoming place that hosts markets and has a hostel and sauna.

343 **2 WILLOW ROAD**

2 Willow Road
NW3 1TH
North ⑩
+44 (0)20 7435 6166
www.nationaltrust.org.
uk/2-willow-road

This 1939 terraced house in Hampstead was designed by the architect Ernő Goldfinger, who lived here until his death in 1987. Hugely influential, it's the only modernist house open to the public and is a superb example, featuring a spiral staircase deigned by Ove Arup and a spacious interior with bespoke furniture and 20th-century artworks by Bridget Riley, Marcel Duchamp and Henry Moore.

344 **ECONOMIST BUILDING**

25 St James's St
SW1A 1HG
Mayfair ⑧

These offices built for The Economist magazine in 1962-4 by British architects Alison and Peter Smithson are located amongst the private galleries and antiquarian book dealers of St James's. Exemplifying the 'new brutalism' the designs are simple and restrained but have a bold, straightforward construction of Portland sandstone and exposed steel on a raised pedestrian courtyard.

345 **BARBICAN ESTATE**

City of London
Silk Street
EC2Y 8DS
Clerkenwell ②

These concrete towers and terrace blocks, built in the 1960s and 70s and designed in the 50s, are prominent and successful examples of brutalism. Built in an area devastated by bombing, The Barbican is a utopian experiment for city living conceived along Corbusian lines. It incorporates courtyards, green spaces, public walkways and cultural enterprises.

YOUR CONSCIENCE

REDCHURCH STREET

40 PLACES
TO DISCOVER
CONTEMPORARY
LONDON

————

5 of the hippest
HANGOUTS

346 **OSLO**
1a Amhurst Road
E8 1LL
Hackney ⑨
+44 (0)20 3553 4831
www.oslohackney.com

This multi-purpose venue is housed in a stylishly renovated former railway building next to Hackney Central station. There's a hip Nordic aesthetic, especially in the restaurant. A relaxed bar area serves craft ales including from Five Points in Hackney Wick. Upstairs there's a live music venue showcasing the latest bands whilst downstairs is a club.

347 **DOVER STREET MARKET**
18-22 Haymarket
SW1Y 4DG
Soho ①
+44 (0)20 7518 0680
www.doverstreetmarket. com

DSM is an upmarket, cutting-edge fashion concept store founded by Rei Kawakubo of Comme des Garçons. Over four storeys it features dozens of haute designer labels, collaborations, pop-ups and some very creative visual merchandising. Concessions also include the excellent IDEA books, Labour and Wait and the Rose Bakery cafe.

348 LONDON FIELDS

West Side
E8 3EU
Hackney ⑨

On a warm and sunny day London Fields is the place to be. It's a popular spot for east Londoner's to come and relax. There's lots of green space and plenty of facilities including the lido, cricket pitch, BBQ area, flower meadow, play areas and the Pub on the Park. On Sundays there's a farmers market.

349 SPIRITLAND

9-10 Stable St
N1C 4AB
Bloomsbury ②
+44 (0)20 3319 0050
www.spiritland.com

A haven for audiophile music lovers, Spiritland is a buzzy new cafe and bar that boasts a bespoke world-class sound system rumoured to have cost hundreds of thousands of pounds. It is host to events, talks, gigs and sets from deep digging DJs and record collectors, as well as a shop selling vinyl, books and musical equipment.

350 GOODHOOD

151 Curtain Road
EC2A 3QE
East ③
+44 (0) 20 7729 3600
www.goodhoodstore.com

This fashion concept store is a great place to discover new trends. The ground floor has an excellent multi-branded selection of men's and women's clothing, plus a range of books and magazines. The basement houses a lifestyle selection including kitchenware, textiles, ceramics, toys, beauty products and camping accessories.

5 notable
21ST-CENTURY BUILDINGS

---

351 AQUATICS CENTRE

Olympic Park
E20 2ZQ
Hackney ⑨
+44 (0)20 8536 3150
*www.londonaquatics
centre.org*

Zaha Hadid's world-class swimming pool and aquatics building was completed for the 2012 Olympics, winning a shortlisting for the prestigious RIBA Sterling Prize. The concept was inspired by the fluid geometry of water in motion. The pool is now open to the public at very accessible prices.
The velodrome in the park – known as 'the Pringle' – is worth a look too.

352 DARBISHIRE PLACE

Bethnal Green
E1 8PN
East ③

This social housing block commissioned by Peabody Housing was completed in 2014 and shortlisted for the RIBA Sterling Prize. Niall McLaughlin Architects were able to successfully complement the Victorian mansion blocks that stood in the same square, with a design that was at once restrained, practical, economical and beautiful.

353 UNICORN THEATRE FOR CHILDREN

147 Tooley St
SE1 2HZ
Southbank ④
www.unicorntheatre.com

This purpose-built children's theatre, the largest of its kind in the country, was designed by Keith Williams and completed in 2005, winning a RIBA award. It's a successful building that comprises two theatre spaces and a cafe. It has a bold, dramatic and colourful asymmetrical design with the interior being visible to the public from the street.

354 TATE MODERN GALLERY EXTENSION

Bankside
SE1 9TG
Southbank ④
www.tate.org.uk/visit/
tate-modern

Completed in 2016 the dramatic ten-storey extension to the Tate Modern gallery has hugely expanded the exhibition space. Herzog and de Meuron have designed the distinctive new building, which is connected to the main galleries by a walkway over the Turbine Hall. The top floor has a public terrace with 360-degree views of the city.

355 EXHIBITION ROAD

South Kensington
SW7 2DD
South West ⑥
www.rbkc.gov.uk/subsites/
exhibitionroad.aspx

Not an actual building but a significant and successful redesign project by Architects Dixon and Jones of this grand street in the museum district. The concept was to simplify and de-clutter the urban environment, creating a civilised, kerb-free shared space for pedestrians and road users.

The 5 most revealing
FREE VIEWPOINTS

---

356 PRIMROSE HILL
Primrose Hill Road
NW3 3NA
North ⑩

Primrose Hill is a grass parkland which lies just to the north of the much bigger Regent's Park. There's a wonderful view south across central London. It's adjacent to the attractive and prosperous neighbourhood of the same name, and to London Zoo. A stone at the summit quotes William Blake: "I have conversed with the spiritual sun. I saw him on Primrose Hill."

357 WATERLOO BRIDGE
WC2R 2PP
Southbank ④

This elegant bridge affords the best and most dramatic ground-level view of London. To the west are the Houses of Parliament, Big Ben and Whitehall. To the east stand the towers of the Barbican and the City, and the dome of St Paul's. To the south the Royal Festival Hall, the National Theatre and London Eye. To the north Somerset House, the Savoy Hotel and the Shell Building. The restless, murky river surges beneath you.

358 RICHMOND PARK

TW10 5HX
(overview map)
*www.royalparks.org.uk/
parks/richmond-park*

This wonderful 17th-century deer park is London's largest green space. From Sawyer's Hill there are great views to central London with the London Eye and Gherkin visible, and from King Henry's Mound near Pembroke Lodge is a famous protected view to St Paul's Cathedral. The vista was created in 1710 and is framed by a cut through trees in the park.

359 GREENWICH OBSERVATORY

Blackheath Avenue
Greenwich Park
SE10 8XJ
(overview map)
+44 (0)20 8858 4422
*www.rmg.co.uk/
royal-observatory*

The view from on top of the hill outside the Observatory offers the finest natural vista in London. Standing on the Meridian Line the view south to Maritime Greenwich and beyond is stunning, especially at dusk. The view takes in Greenwich Park, the beautiful National Maritime Museum and Old Royal Navy College buildings, the Thames, Docklands, Canary Wharf's skyscrapers and the City.

360 TATE MODERN

Bankside
SE1 9TG
Southbank ④
*www.tate.org.uk/visit/
tate-modern*

The new Switch House extension at Tate Modern is ten stories high and has a public viewing terrace from where there are excellent 360-degree views right across London. From the sixth floor the original power station building has a superb view directly across the river to St Paul's and the City.

The 5 best
SIGHTSEEING TRIPS
by public transport

---

361 DOCKLANDS LIGHT RAILWAY
www.tfl.gov.uk/modes/dlr

The DLR is a driverless light metro system that mostly runs on an elevated line above ground, serving the Docklands area in east London. Take the route from Bank station to Greenwich. This takes in parts of the East End, the skyscrapers and docks of the Canary Wharf business district, and on to historic Greenwich.

362 NUMBER 9 BUS
www.tfl.gov.uk/bus/route/9

The number 9 bus route begins outside Somerset House at Aldwych and proceeds to take in some of London's best known sights. Trafalgar Square, Piccadilly, Green Park, Hyde Park, Royal Albert Hall and Kensington Palace are all on the itinerary before you reach the upmarket Kensington High Street shopping district.

363 THAMES CLIPPERS

www.thamesclippers.com

This riverboat bus service accepts Oyster cards and also offers a River Roamer ticket allowing all-day travel on the Thames. Their high-speed catamarans are an excellent and affordable way to see London from the river. You can travel from Putney in the west to Greenwich in the east and they also run the service between Tate Britain and Tate Modern.

364 NUMBER 11 BUS

www.tfl.gov.uk/bus/route/11

This route begins at Liverpool Street station. Grab the seats at the front of the upper deck and enjoy the ride which takes in the Bank of England, St Paul's Cathedral, Ludgate Circus, Fleet Street, Trafalgar Square, Horse Guards Parade, Whitehall, Downing Street, Parliament Square, the Houses of Parliament, Big Ben and Westminster Abbey before going on to Sloane Square for the King's Road and Saatchi Gallery.

365 LONDON OVERGROUND LOOP

www.tfl.gov.uk/modes/london-overground

Recent extensions to London's Overground rail network (the 'Ginger Line') have created a loop that encircles the familiar central area and explores outlying towns and districts of the city. It's a fascinating journey around some of the inner hinterlands. The route takes in Shepherd's Bush, Hampstead, Highbury, Wapping, Peckham and Chelsea Harbour amongst many other destinations.

The 5 best intimate
NIGHTCLUBS
for underground music

366 THE PICKLE FACTORY
13-14 The Oval
E2 9DU
Hackney ⑨
+44 (0)20 7183 4422
www.thepicklefactory.co.uk

One of London's newest small spaces for dancing, Bethnal Green's Pickle Factory is a 200 capacity club with minimal decor and lighting and an emphasis instead on superior sound and exciting up-and-coming bookings, with parties from the likes of Dream States, Moxie and DJ Sotofett.

367 THE CLF ART CAFE
AKA THE BUSSEY BUILDING
133 Rye Lane
SE15 4ST
South ⑤
+44 (0)20 7732 5275
www.clfartcafe.org

This small warehouse space in Peckham has a broad music policy that includes soul, house, garage, disco and more besides. The South London Soul Train puts on regular nights of soul, funk and disco with live acts. Bump and Hustle Music have a regular house night and there are one-offs specials that may include DJs like Marcellus Pittman, Andrew Ashong and Ge-Ology.

368 CORSICA STUDIOS

4/5 Elephant Road
SE17 1LB
Southbank ④
+44 (0)20 7703 4760
www.corsicastudios.com

Located beneath two railway arches behind Elephant and Castle station, Corsica Studios is a medium-sized club with a cutting-edge, forward-thinking music policy that covers house, techno, bass and disco. The two rooms are stripped back and have a huge sound system. The Columbian next door is an even more intimate dance venue.

369 PHONOX

418 Brixton Road
SW9 7AY
South ⑤
+44 (0)20 7095 9411
www.phonox.co.uk

Opened in 2015 Phonox in Brixton has a great sound system and an ambitious left-field music policy. Friday nights are given over to just one DJ to play all night, featuring artists like Omar-S, MCDE, Skream and Ben UFO. Saturday nights feature the young female resident HAAi playing global house grooves alongside top-level unannounced guests.

370 BRILLIANT CORNERS

470 Kingsland Road
E8 4AE
Hackney ⑨
+44 (0)20 7812 9511
*www.brilliantcorners
london.co.uk*

Far from being a full-on nightclub, Brilliant Corners is nonetheless a wonderful place to hear amazing music in an intimate environment. The bar has a superb audiophile Klipschorn sound system and a mix of expert vinyl selectors playing all styles of music. There's a small dancefloor and a Japanese menu. The music is streamed live on their website and archived.

The 5 best
NEIGHBOURHOODS
to visit

---

371 **STOKE NEWINGTON**
Hackney ⑨

'Stokey', as it is known to locals, has retained its London 'village' feel. Centred round the historic Church Street area there are plenty of independent and distinctive shops and restaurants. The area has a strong community character and there are plenty of green spaces to explore too.

372 **GREENWICH**
(overview map)

Greenwich has many famous historical attractions to offer, but there are plenty of other reasons to visit this lively community, including the excellent markets, the independent shops and restaurants, the Meantime Brewery, the O2 concert venue and the beautiful park.

373 **SHOREDITCH**
East ③

Shoreditch earned its reputation for creative cool in the mid-to-late 1990s. It's still the centre for much of east London's entrepreneurial and cultural activity with many fashionable independent shops, bars, clubs, coffee shops, restaurants and start-up businesses.

374 **RICHMOND**
(Overview map)

An attractive historic town on the river Thames, 8 miles west of central London. There are riverside pubs and restaurants, a good range of high street and independent shops, theatres, an indie cinema, boat trips and a wonderful urban Green. From Richmond Hill is a superb view along the river to Eel Pie Island, and beyond that lies marvellous Richmond Park.

375 **BRIXTON AND HERNE HILL**
South ⑤

Multicultural Brixton has a wealth of exciting attractions, chief among these being the must-visit Brixton Village and the excellent markets, music venues and cinema. Nearby Herne Hill has attractive Brockwell Park with its Lido and cafe, and interesting indie shops and a farmers' market near the station.

373 SHOREDITCH

The 5 best

INDEPENDENT SHOPPING STREETS

---

376 **GOLBORNE ROAD**
W10 5PR
West ⑦

Off the far end of the more famous Portobello Road lies this incredibly cosmopolitan and characterful street that bustles with its engaging mix of independent boutiques, traditional retailers, vintage and antique shops and a wide range of international restaurants. A street market sells bric-a-brac and groceries alongside street food stalls such as the prized Moroccan fish food shack.

377 **LAMB'S CONDUIT STREET**
WC1N 3LL
Bloomsbury ②

This historic and partly pedestrianised street in Bloomsbury is particularly good for menswear and inspiring homewares. Plus there's the Persephone bookshop, a bike shop, the community co-operative People's Supermarket and great cafes, pubs and restaurants.

378 **BERMONDSEY STREET**
SE1 3XF
Southbank ④

White Cube and the Fashion and Textile Museum offer culture, Casse-Croûte, José and The Garrison are a few of the eating options, plus there are great gift shops, boutiques and an antiques market on Fridays.

379 REDCHURCH STREET

E2 7DJ

East ③

Once-gritty Redchurch Street is now host to a range of stylish and distinctive independent shops, galleries, cafes and bars. APC, MHL, Modern Society, Aesop, Klaus Haapaniemi and Tracey Neuls are among the best shops.

380 NEWBURGH STREET

W1F 7RG

Soho ①

There's a network of narrow streets close to Carnaby Street and Oxford Circus that includes Newburgh Street, Marshall Street and Kingly Court that offer a great range of indie shops.

377 LAMB'S CONDUIT STREET

379 REDCHURCH STREET

378 BERMONDSEY STREET

5
WALKS
to discover contemporary London

381 **LIVERPOOL STREET STATION TO DALSTON**
East ③

This walk follows a straight line north from the financial district, through Shoreditch and on to one of London's most vital areas, Dalston. Starting in sight of the Gherkin and Lloyd's building you'll go past Spitalfields Market, Shoreditch Church, the Geffrye Museum Dalston's Ridley Road Market and the Rio Cinema. Continue on to Stoke Newington Church Street if you're feeling energetic.

382 **SOUTHBANK RIVER WALK**
Southbank ④

This walk follows the Thames Path along the river and is one of the most revealing and pleasant in London. Begin outside the Royal Festival Hall and continue east past the Hayward Gallery, BFI cinema and the brutalist National Theatre building. Continue on to Borough Market and Southwark Cathedral, taking in Tate Modern, Shakespeare's Globe Theatre and Clink Street.

383 **MAYFAIR**
Mayfair ⑧

Between Hyde Park to the west and Regent's Street to the east Mayfair is London's most exclusive district, home to its most luxurious shops, hotels and restaurants. A circuitous walk should take in Berkeley and Grosvenor Squares, louche Shepherd's Market, Burlington Arcade, Saville Row, the Royal Academy of Arts and Bond, Brook and Duke Streets for shopping.

384 **HACKNEY**
Hackney ⑨

From Hackney Central station explore along Wilton Way and down through London Fields to Broadway Market, before making your way back via Mentmore Terrace and Mare Street. You'll soon see why this is one of the hippest parts of town, with so many creative new businesses.

385 **WHITECHAPEL TO ST PAUL'S CATHEDRAL**
East ③

Begin in the old East End at Whitechapel station and head west along Whitechapel Road. There's an Asian street market here selling food, fashions and plenty more besides, plus a possible diversion onto the southern, Bangladeshi end of Brick Lane. Continue on to the Whitechapel Gallery, then negotiate Aldgate Circus and continue on through the financial City district, via Leadenhall Market and the Bank of England, to the cathedral.

HORNIMAN MUSEUM

25 THINGS TO DO WITH CHILDREN

———

The 5 best
MUSEUMS FOR CHILDREN

---

386 HORNIMAN MUSEUM
100 London Road
SE23 3PQ
South ⑤
+44 (0)20 8699 1872
www.horniman.ac.uk

The Horniman Museum specialises in natural history, anthropology and musical instruments. There are many stuffed animals including a walrus. The huge garden has a nature trail and there's also an aquarium, beehive and the Hands On Base area.

387 RAGGED SCHOOL MUSEUM
46-50 Copperfield Road
E3 4RR
East ⑨
+44 (0)20 8980 6405
www.raggedschool
museum.org.uk

Ragged Schools were charitable institutions providing free education to the poor during the Victorian era. This fascinating building was once such a school and recreates the Victorian educational experience, including a typical classroom and displays about East End childhood and local history.

388 V&A MUSEUM OF CHILDHOOD
Cambridge Heath Road
E2 9PA
East ③
+44 (0)20 8983 5200
www.vam.ac.uk/moc

The V&A's sister museum in Bethnal Green holds the largest collection of children's toys in the country. In each area there's an activity station to engage children, as well as a sandpit, board games to play and a book corner with storytelling.

389 LONDON TRANSPORT MUSEUM

Covent Garden Piazza
WC2E 7BB
Covent Garden ①
+44 (0)20 7379 6344
www.ltmuseum.co.uk

This child-friendly museum tells the story of public transport in London since 1800. There are many vehicles to explore and interact with and there's a play area and a fleet of mini vehicles to ride. For parents there are good displays on the design history of London Transport.

390 IMPERIAL WAR MUSEUM

Lambeth Road
SE1 6HZ
Southbank ④
+44 (0)20 7416 5000
www.iwm.org.uk/visits/
iwm-london

The IWM has a large atrium full of guns and tanks with aircraft hanging from the ceiling, including a Spitfire and Harrier jet. Beyond this there are some thought-provoking and creative displays on both the front line and the home front during the World Wars. The Holocaust and Crimes Against Humanity displays are recommended for older children only.

386 HORNIMAN MUSEUM

5
ADVENTUROUS PLACES
to visit with children

---

391 KEW GARDENS TREETOP WALKWAY

47 Kew Green
TW9 3AB
South West ⑥
+44 (0)20 8332 5655
www.kew.org

The treetop walkway gives a spectacular bird's-eye view out over the beautiful arboretum at Kew. At 18 metres high, with 118 steps up and a 200-metre circular route amongst the tree canopy, it's a real adventure. Kew also has the world's biggest Victorian greenhouse with its own walkway, an aquarium, a bee garden and a botanical play area called Climbers and Creepers.

392 NATIONAL CENTRE FOR CIRCUS ARTS

Coronet St
N1 6HD
East ③
+44 (0) 20 7613 4141
www.nationalcircus.org.uk

This professional training centre for circus performers is an amazing place for children to come to learn circus skills. They offer a Youth Circus Experience Day for 8-16 year olds where trapeze, diabolo, tight wire and juggling skills are taught. Longer term courses teach flying trapeze and acrobatics, and there's also a Family Circus course for younger accompanied children.

393 HOLLAND PARK ADVENTURE PLAYGROUND

100 Holland Park Avenue
W11 4UA
West ⑦

This adventure playground is in one of London's best green spaces. The facilities are extensive and include a zip wire, giant seesaw, rope swings, a climbing wall, rope walks, climbing frames and an aerial walkway. There's a separate fenced-in area for younger children. The park also has woodland areas, peacocks and a cafe.

394 MUDLARKING ON THE THAMES

Southbank ④

A 'mudlark' is an 18th-century term for someone who scavenges in the river mud. On the South Bank between the National and Globe Theatres are a few places where the river shore can be accessed at low tide. Anything could turn up on each tide such as ceramics, jewellery and old coins. Digging is not allowed without a licence and any significant finds should be reported to the Museum of London.

395 BAYSIXTY6 SKATE PARK

Bay 66 - Acklam Road
W10 5QZ
West ⑦
+44 (0) 20 8960 6713
www.baysixty6.com

This large indoor skate park under the Westway in Notting Hill is a fantastic place for either experienced or beginner skaters. The facilities are superb with many ramps, rails, pipes and ledges to negotiate. Day passes and beginner lessons are offered, and the equipment is available to hire or buy.

The 5 best
SHOPS FOR KIDS

396 OLIVE LOVES ALFIE

84 Stoke Newington
Church St
N16 0AP
Hackney ⑨
+44 (0)20 7241 4212
www.olivelovesalfie.co.uk

This 'creative family store' is a neighbourhood favourite, selling clothing and shoes for babies, toddlers and children. They also stock a stylish collection of beautifully illustrated books as well as toys, games, crafts and homewares. All products have lasting hand-me-down appeal and quality.

397 BENJAMIN POLLOCK'S TOY SHOP

44 The Market
WC2E 8RF
Covent Garden ①
+44 (0)20 7379 7866
www.pollocks-coventgarden.
co.uk

Pollock's dates back to the 1850s and the stock of this delightfully traditional shop has changed remarkably little. They specialise in beautiful toy theatres, dioramas and shadow boxes as well as puppets, masks, music boxes and pocket money novelties.

398 TALES ON MOON LANE

25 Half Moon Lane
SE24 9JU
South ⑤
+44 (0)20 7274 5759
www.talesonmoonlane.co.uk

Award-winning Tales on Moon Lane is one of the best specialist children's bookshops in the country. The window displays are imaginative and inspiring, there's a wide range of well-chosen stock for all ages, and the staff are friendly and expert.

399 THE TOYBOX

223 Victoria Park Road
E9 7HD
Hackney ⑨
+44 (0)20 8533 2879
www.thetoyboxshop.co.uk

Handily located next to Victoria Park, one of east London's best green spaces, The Toybox is loved for its great range of unusual and alternative toy ideas. They sell a wide mix of traditional and very contemporary toys for creative fun including fishing sets, puppets, soft toys, Lego, wooden toys, kites and inexpensive pocket money items.

400 LA COQUETA

5 Heath St
NW3 6TP
North ⑩
+44 (0)20 7435 1875
www.lacoquetakids.com

Mother of five Celia Muñoz set up this clothing boutique in Hampstead after noticing how much love her children's Spanish clothes were getting on London's streets. La Coqueta only sells high quality, chic and traditional clothing and shoes made in Spain. She works with Spanish designers to create functional, hard-wearing and stylish products for ages 0-7.

398 TALES ON MOON LANE

5 inspiring
THINGS TO DO
with children

401 **SERPENTINE GALLERY SUMMER PAVILION**

Kensington Gardens
W2 3XA
South West ⑥
+44 (0)20 7402 6075
www.serpentine
galleries.org

Each summer the Serpentine Gallery in Hyde Park commissions an international architect to build an exciting temporary structure that's to include a social space and cafe. Some of the world's greatest architects have taken part, creating inspirational buildings. It's a great place to take kids to explore architecture, to see art and to have a picnic in the park.

402 **SHAKESPEARE'S GLOBE**

21 New Globe Walk
Bankside
SE1 9DT
Southbank ④
+44 (0)20 7902 1400
www.shakespearesglobe.com

On the South Bank next to Tate Modern is a reconstruction of Shakespeare's 1599 theatre: a three-tiered open-air wooden structure where performances are 'in the round.' Entrance includes a tour which explores the amazing building, Shakespeare's work and the London of his lifetime. There's a Family Trail and Groundling theatre tickets (standing by the stage) are only £5.

403 CENTRE OF THE CELL

4 Newark St
E1 2AT
East ③
+44 (0)20 7882 2562
www.centreofthecell.org

Queen Mary University runs this innovative project which aims to inspire curiosity for science in the young. Suspended above a working biomedical research laboratory is an orange pod that's accessed by a glass-walled walkway. Inside children will learn about the amazing world of human cells and the human body through interactive games, films and talking with experts.

404 BIG FISH LITTLE FISH

www.bigfishlittlefish
events.co.uk

Since 2013 BFLF have organised daytime raves ('2-4 hour party people') for young children and families that are great fun, highly social and a little anarchic. They run irregular events at unusual venues across town, often with themes like 'Superheroes in Space.' Renowned club DJs provide the tunes whilst bubble machines, workshops, glowsticks, balloons and face painting provide further entertainment.

405 CLIMB THE MONUMENT

Fish St Hill/Monument St
EC3R 8AH
City ④
www.themonument.info

At 62 metres high The Monument is the tallest isolated stone column in the world. It was erected shortly after the 1666 Great Fire of London, close to the start of the fire in Pudding Lane. Climbing the 311 spiral steps and gaining the panoramic view of the city is an exhilarating experience, especially for a child.

5 places for
OUTDOOR FUN

---

406 BATTERSEA PARK CHILDREN'S ZOO

Chelsea Bridge Gate
SW11 4NJ
South West ⑥
+44 (0)20 7924 5826
www.batterseaparkzoo.co.uk

The zoo at Battersea Park is modestly sized and features a good range of smaller animals, making it an ideal day out for younger children. As well as the animal attractions there's an adventure playground, sandpit and a cafe. Elsewhere in the park there are river views, a boating lake and the Go Ape Tree Top Adventure.

407 LONDON WETLAND CENTRE

Queen Elizabeth's Walk
SW13 9WT
West ⑦
+44 (0)20 8409 4400
www.wwt.org.uk/wetland-centres/london

It may seem hard to believe that central London has a significant wetland area. There are lakes, marshes, ponds and trails to explore, plus an indoor discovery centre, adventure playground and cafe. The World Wetlands area has exotic wildfowl and otters you can get up close to.

408 HACKNEY CITY FARM

1a Goldsmiths Row
E2 8QA
Hackney ⑨
+44 (0)20 7729 6381
www.hackneycityfarm.co.uk

Entry to this community city farm is free and there are many animals to see up close including pigs, sheep, rabbits and donkeys. Pottery and woodcraft sessions are available and they also run baby music classes and a young farmers' club.

09 OUTDOOR PARKOUR CLASSES

www.parkourgenerations. com

Parkour is an energetic combination of running, climbing, vaulting and other movements around obstacles in urban spaces. The first ever outdoor classes in London are run by Parkour Generation, who have a weekly youth session in different parts of town for ages 7-15.

10 BMX AT THE OLYMPIC VELO PARK

Queen Elizabeth
Olympic Park
Abercrombie Road
E20 3AB
Hackney ⑨

Riding a BMX bike around the berms, bumps and jumps of this track is an exhilarating experience. Taster sessions for beginners, where key skills and techniques are taught, are available and there are also pay and ride sessions for more experienced riders. Equipment is available for hire.

408 HACKNEY CITY FARM

BERT'S BARGES

20 PLACES
TO SLEEP

The 5 hippest
DESIGN HOTELS

---

411 ACE HOTEL

100 Shoreditch High St
E1 6JA
East ③
+44 (0)20 7613 9800
www.acehotel.com/london

Hip hotel chain Ace chose the creative melting pot of Shoreditch as the site for their first opening outside the US. It has a stylish contemporary industrial interior and ticks off plenty of hipster wishes such as its own coffee shop, basement club, gallery, juice bar, flower shop and even a branch of Sister Ray record shop.

412 CHARLOTTE STREET HOTEL

15-17 Charlotte St
W1T 1RJ
Bloomsbury ②
+44 (0)20 7806 2000
www.firmdalehotels.com/
hotels/london/charlotte
street-hotel

Designer Kit Kemp created this gorgeous boutique in Fitzrovia, perfect for explorations into the West End or Bloomsbury. The bohemian Bloomsbury Group and their Omega Workshops of a century ago are the inspiration for the interior styling, including original paintings by Duncan Grant and Vanessa Bell. The beautifully appointed Oscar cocktail bar and restaurant is usually buzzing.

413 ZETTER TOWNHOUSE

86-88 St John's Square
EC1V 4JJ
Clerkenwell ②
+44 (0)20 7324 4567
www.thezettertownhouse.
com/clerkenwell

This Georgian townhouse hotel is well situated in a hip part of town, with plenty of great restaurants close by. Having only 13 rooms the warm, stylish and old-fashioned eccentricity of the interiors give it the feeling of being a private residence. The cocktail bar is award-winning and certainly worth a visit in itself.

414 TOWN HALL HOTEL

Patriot Square
E2 9NF
East ③
+44 (0)20 7871 0460
www.townhallhotel.com

Historic Bethnal Green Town Hall dates from 1910 and is a grand, imposing building in the art deco style. It has recently been transformed into a very fine hotel. The new interiors have retained many of the period features but have a bright modern feel. The Typing Room restaurant and Peg and Patriot bar are worth a look too.

415 THE CULPEPER

40 Commercial St
E1 6LP
East ③
+44 (0)20 7247 5371
www.theculpeper.com

More than just a hotel, The Culpeper near to Brick Lane is a large red-brick Victorian building that's home to a fine pub with craft ales on its ground floor, a lauded restaurant on its first floor, and five very reasonably priced rooms on the upper floor. These share a stylish, stripped-back aesthetic with the rest of the building. The roof terrace has a garden and greenhouse where you can take breakfast.

5
AFFORDABLE PLACES
to sleep

416 YHA ST PAUL'S

36 Carter Lane
EC4V 5AB
City ④
+44 (0)845 371 9012
www.yha.org.uk/hostel/
london-st-pauls

Youth Hostels are not only for youths – anyone can stay in this historic building, a former school for the choirboys at St Paul's Cathedral. Full of interesting period features and with an elaborate exterior, this is a great place to stay in such a central location. Facilities are comfortable but basic, with beds from £16, private rooms from £30 and family rooms from £35.

417 AVO HOTEL

82 Dalston Lane
E8 3AH
Hackney ⑨
+44 (0)20 3490 5061
www.avohotel.com

Avo is a family-run, eco-friendly hotel with a warm welcome in the hip and lively Dalston area. Rooms are compact but stylish, with Egyptian cotton bedding and other little extras that give it a boutique feel despite being very reasonably priced, with double rooms from £69.

118 CITIZENM LONDON

20 Lavington St
SE1 0NZ
Southbank ④
+44 (0)20 3519 1680
www.citizenm.com

The London outpost of this small international chain of stylish budget hotels is in a great location between Tate Modern and Borough Market. The rooms are small but comfortable and well designed. The ground floor is open-plan and has a colourful and quirky modern interior with Vitra furniture, a bar, canteen, library and relaxed seating area.

119 CLINK 78

78 King's Cross Road
WC1X 9QG
Clerkenwell ②
+44 (0)20 7183 9400
www.clinkhostels.com/
london/clink78

Housed in a former magistrates' court building, this hostel near King's Cross offers stylish and affordable accommodation for backpackers and budget travellers. There's a late night bar in the basement, a film lounge and many other facilities. The original heavy-doored prison cells that give Clink 78 its name are available to sleep in, as well as the dorms and private rooms.

120 THE HOOTANANNY

95 Effra Road
SW2 1DF
South ⑤
+44 (0)20 7737 7273
www.hootanannyhostel.
co.uk

Above The Hootananny pub in Brixton is a great value hostel. The lively 'dub pub' is an award-winning live music venue specialising in reggae, dub, international funk and soul styles, hip-hop and also comedy acts. The hostel facilities are basic, but in a good location, comfortable and very reasonably priced.

5

UNUSUAL PLACES

to sleep

---

421 BERT'S BARGES

Bert's luxury floating barge is moored up on a quiet and pretty stretch of the Regent's Canal. The interiors are incredibly stylish, with a modern Scandinavian feel. The barge is equipped with a wood burning stove, underground heating, king size bed and has a roof terrace.

422 40 WINKS

Renowned interior designer David Carter invites you to enjoy 40 Winks at his own residence, a 'micro-boutique' hotel with only two rooms. Entering his historic 1717 house near Stepney Green in east London is to encounter a magical atmosphere, each room having its own distinctive, unique character.

423 GIR LION LODGE
AT ZSL LONDON ZOO

Ever fancied a sleepover at the zoo? Well now it's possible to stay within roaring distance of the asiatic lions (and other animals) at London Zoo in one of nine colourful Gujarati-style wooden lodges. The unique experience includes torchlight and early morning tours complete with animal interactions.

124 GOOD HOTEL

Royal Victoria Dock
Western Gateway
E16 1FA
East
+44 (0)20 3637 7401
www.goodhotellondon.com

This large floating hotel in the Docklands was a Dutch detention centre before it crossed the channel. On the trip over it gained smart industrial interiors, cosy cabin-like rooms, a roof terrace garden with a bar, and a relaxed communal vibe. Reasonably priced, the Good Hotel works with the local community to train the unemployed.

125 THE GEORGIAN HOUSE

Hampton Court Palace
Hampton Court
www.landmarktrust.org.uk/
search-and-book/properties/
georgian-house-7805

Remarkably, the Landmark Trust rents out an apartment within the grounds of the Hampton Court Palace residence of King Henry VIII, in an imposing and elegant 1719 brick house that was once the Prince of Wales's kitchen. Guests are free to walk the extensive and magnificent gardens and courtyards, and will glimpse Palace life beyond the public's gaze.

421 BERT'S BARGES

5 of the most
CHARMING HOTELS

426 HAZLITT'S

6 Frith St
W1D 3JA
Soho ①
+44 (0)20 7434 1771
www.hazlittshotel.com

A boutique hotel of particular charm, named after essayist William Hazlitt, whose dying words "well, I've lived a happy life" were uttered in these very premises. It's wonderfully located near to Soho Square. The four-storey townhouse buildings have 30 rooms, all individually designed with traditional furnishings and antiques, with 2.000 paintings and prints on display in total.

427 THE FOX AND ANCHOR

115 Charterhouse St
EC1M 6AA
Clerkenwell ②
+44 (0)20 7250 1300
www.foxandanchor.com

A Victorian public house overlooking historic Smithfield Market, the Fox and Anchor is a terrific all-rounder. It offers fine ales, superior gastro pub food and has atmospheric dark-wooden interiors, on top of which are six beautifully appointed rooms. Add in the famously hearty breakfasts they provide to the local market workers and you have a winning combination.

428 ARLINGTON AVENUE B&B

26 Arlington Avenue
N1 7AX
Islington ①
+44 (0)7711 265 183
www.arlingtonavenue.co.uk

A private residence in a 1948 building, located between Islington and Hackney and close to the Regent's Canal, this atmospheric B&B has only two rooms to let, a double and a single. The hospitality is personal and considered, the interiors refined and attractive. It's also incredibly reasonably priced.

429 ARTIST RESIDENCE

52 Cambridge St
SW1V 4QQ
South West ⑥
+44 (0)20 7931 8946
www.artistresidencelondon.co.uk

Recently opened, this award-winning and cosy ten-room boutique hotel in Pimlico is well situated for trips to Chelsea and Tate Britain. All the rooms in this former Victorian pub are individually and eclectically designed. The relaxing clubroom features a fire place, ensuring a warm welcome. Other attractions include a games room, kitchen cafe and basement cocktail bar.

430 THE ROOKERY HOTEL

12 Peter's Lane
Cowcross Street
EC1M 6DS
Clerkenwell ②
+44 (0)20 7336 0931
www.rookeryhotel.com

Occupying a pair of 18th-century townhouses in the fashionable Farringdon area, The Rookery offers atmospheric and romantic rooms with an old-world charm – think open fires, antique furniture, wood panelled walls and heaving bookshelves. There's a secret garden and at the top of the building is the Rook's Nest, a huge split-level apartment with a view of St Paul's.

RICHMOND PARK

35 WEEKEND ACTIVITIES

5 places to
SWIM OUTSIDE

431 BROCKWELL PARK LIDO
Brockwell Park
Dulwich Road
SE24 0PA
South ⑤
+44 (0)20 7274 3088

Built in 1937 at the height of Britain's first love affair with outdoor swimming, this Lido is a Grade II listed art deco example in attractive Brockwell Park. The pool is Olympic-sized at 50 metres long and opens all-year-round. It's very popular in the summer, as is the award-winning Lido Cafe.

432 LONDON FIELDS LIDO
London Fields - West Side
E8 3EU
Hackney ⑨
+44 (0)20 7254 9038

Saved from demolition as recently as 2006, this pool is now a popular attraction in east London. It's London's only Olympic-sized heated outdoor pool. Floodlights have recently been installed to extend the winter opening hours.

433 OASIS SPORTS CENTRE
32 Endell St
WC2H 9AG
Covent Garden ①
+44 (0)20 7831 1804

This council-owned Covent Garden pool really is an oasis in the city. The outdoor pool is on a sunny rooftop, 27.5 metres long and heated all-year-round. Other facilities include an indoor pool and an extensive range of gym equipment, plus a cafe and sun terrace.

34 THE SERPENTINE LIDO

Hyde Park
W2 2UH
South West ⑥
+44 (0)20 7706 3422

A large curved lake in the middle of Hyde Park, the Serpentine was used for the 2012 Olympic triathlon events, and has a dedicated area for wild swimming. The water is unheated and unchlorinated, with the partitioned area for swimming measuring 30 by 100 metres. It's open to the general public only in the summer months.

35 HAMPSTEAD HEATH PONDS

Hampstead
NW5 1QR
North ⑩
+44 (0)20 7485 3873

The large ancient parkland of Hampstead Heath, with its extensive woodland and superb views down to the city, is home to three swimming ponds. The Ladies', Men's and Mixed Ponds, spread out across the heath, offer the closest thing to a rural swim in London.

431 BROCKWELL PARK LIDO

The 5 best
HIDDEN GARDENS

---

436 KYOTO GARDEN

112-114 Holland Park
Avenue
W11 4UA
West ⑦
+44 (0)20 7361 3003

Hidden within the leafy confines of Holland Park is this serene Japanese-style garden created in 1991. The design is typical of Japanese gardens with a pretty landscaped area that features a waterfall, stone bridge and a pond with large koi fish swimming around.

437 LINCOLN'S INN FIELDS

WC2A 3TL
City ④
+44 (0)20 7974 1693

Laid out in the 1630s, this is London's largest and arguably finest public square. It's a large green space that's surrounded on all sides by historic buildings and institutions, giving it a cloistered atmosphere. At the eastern side is the brick gatehouse to Lincoln's Inn Court.

438 CHELSEA PHYSIC GARDEN

66 Royal Hospital Road
SW3 4HS
South West ⑥
+44 (0)20 7352 5646
*www.chelseaphysicgarden.
co.uk*

This is a tranquil and magical place. It was founded in 1673 and is England's second oldest botanical garden. Originally an apothecary garden, it remains an important place for the study of medicinal plants. It closes during the winter except for a short window when the snowdrops come into flower.

39 V&A MADEJSKI GARDEN

Cromwell Road
SW7 2RL
South West ⑥
+44 (0)20 7942 2000

In the heart of the V&A's museum is this superb courtyard garden. It's a delightful space, surrounded on all sides by the imposing 19th-century Italianate museum buildings. Redesigned in 2005 the main feature is a large oval stone pool with fountains, grass areas and hydrangeas and lemon trees planted by the walls.

40 DALSTON EASTERN CURVE GARDEN

13 Dalston Lane
E8 3DF
Hackney ⑨
www.dalstongarden.org

Occupying a formerly derelict space where the Eastern Curve railway line once ran, this community garden is a surprising delight. There are many wildlife-friendly plants and trees, some of which were already growing on the site when the garden was developed in 2009. It has an allotment area, a wooden pavilion for events and an excellent cafe.

437 LINCOLN'S INN FIELDS

LINCOLN'S INN FIELDS WC2
CITY OF WESTMINSTER

The 5 best
BIKE RIDES

---

441 RICHMOND PARK

www.parkcycle.co.uk
(overview map)

London's biggest and wildest park is a fantastic place for cycling. A tarmacked 7-mile loop has a varied and surprisingly hilly terrain, making for a popular training circuit for road cyclists. Running outside that is another loop of off-road trail. All types of bikes including tandems are available for hire from next to the cafe at Roehampton Gate.

442 REGENT'S CANAL

Islington ⑪

Riding alongside the Regent's Canal from Little Venice in Maida Vale to Limehouse in east London is a pleasant and gentle 12-mile off-road route with riverside views all the way. The route takes in Regent's Park, Camden Lock, Islington, Hackney and Victoria Park, the Olympic Park and the Lee Valley before reaching the Thames.

13 DUNWICH DYNAMO

*www.southwarkcyclists.
org.uk/category/events/
dunwich-dynamo-2*

The 'Dun Run' is a legendary informal annual ride that begins at London Fields in Hackney. Cyclists set off at dusk and ride through the night to the tiny village of Dunwich on the Suffolk coast, 115 miles away. It's a friendly, non-competitive event and an exhilarating and rewarding experience.

14 CRITICAL MASS

*www.network23.org/
criticalmasslondon*

The Critical Mass ride takes place on the last Friday of every month. Cyclists meet under Waterloo Bridge in the early evening before taking off on an unorganised ride with an ambiguous purpose but it's an opportunity to ride in a community group and 'reclaim' the streets from traffic for a short while. This can occasionally lead to antagonism from motorists, but the ride is fun and a little anarchic.

15 TALLY HO! CYCLE TOURS

www.tallyhocycletours.com

By bicycle is one of the best ways to explore and discover London. A safe and fun way to do it is with tour company Tally Ho!, which is run by a small group of cycle (and vintage, beer and beard) enthusiasts. They lead a range of engaging and informative rides that take in the sights, history and culture of the city. There even is a 'Gin and Food' tour.

5 fun
WEEKEND ESCAPES

446 WHITSTABLE

www.seewhitstable.com

Only 1.15 hours from London on the train, Whitstable is an historic town on the north Kent coast, famous for its oysters and seafood. There are many good restaurants but try the quaint 150 year-old Wheelers Oyster Bar or The Sportsman, a must-visit gastropub for foodies. The town also has a castle, harbour, beach, art galleries and many quirky independent shops.

447 LEWES

www.visitsussex.org/page/lewes

Lewes is an attractive historic town in the South Downs National Park in Sussex, an hour from London by train. Attractions include a castle, a ruined priory, the Harvey's brewery and plenty of independent shops on the 'twittens' - ancient, steep, cobbled lanes.

48 MARGATE

For years Margate had a reputation as a down-on-its-luck seaside resort, but in 2011 the prestigious Turner Contemporary gallery opened and in 2015 the derelict 1920s Dreamland pleasure resort was reopened, with its many retro amusements including Britain's oldest rollercoaster. Just an hour and a half away by train, it offers quirky shopping, an awe-inspiring shell grotto and real traditional seaside appeal.

49 BATH

www.visitbath.co.uk

An historic spa town in the West Country county of Somerset, Bath is a UNESCO World Heritage Site. As well as the 2000 year-old Roman spa there's the modern Thermae Bath Spa. Factor in the famous Georgian architecture and attractions like the Fashion Museum and it's an hour and a half trip worth taking.

50 SUFFOLK COAST

The quiet and remote Suffolk coast has a subtle but real attraction, and is a designated Area of Outstanding Natural Beauty. The historic coastal towns of Orford, Aldeburgh and Southwold are well known for their fine pubs, restaurants, beaches, beautiful surrounding countryside and unique atmosphere.

5 ADVENTUROUS ACTIVITIES

to try

---

451 THAMES RIB EXPERIENCE

Embankment Pier
Victoria Embankment
WC2N 6NU
Covent Garden ①
+44 (0)20 3613 2338
www.thamesribexperience.
com

Taking to the Thames on a rigid inflatable speedboat is an exhilarating experience. From the Embankment you can take a choice of trips to Tower Bridge, Canary Wharf or as far as the Thames Barrier past Greenwich. The journey starts at a slower pace, before the 740 horsepower engine lets rip for an invigorating burst over the water.

452 THE CASTLE CLIMBING WALL

Green Lanes
N4 2HA
Islington ⑪
+44 (0)20 8211 1082
www.castle-climbing.co.uk

A huge facility based in an impressive former Victorian water-pumping station. The Castle is one of the finest indoor climbing centres in Europe. With over 5 large floors there are more than 450 courses to try at heights of up to 13m, plus bouldering surfaces and descents to abseil from.

153 LEE VALLEY WHITE WATER CENTRE

Station Road
Waltham Cross
EN9 1AB
Hackney ⑨
+44 (0)30 0003 0616
www.gowhitewater.co.uk

One of the best and most exciting legacies of the 2012 Olympics is this White Water Centre located just outside the M25, within the extensive Lee Valley Park that stretches from central London out to Hertfordshire. The man-made rapids are fantastic fun and perfect for White Water rafting, slalom canoeing, kayaking and hydrospeeding.

154 THE CAPITAL RING

www.tfl.gov.uk/modes/walking/capital-ring

Walking the 78-mile Capital Ring offers a discreet kind of adventure. The well-marked orbital route around inner London takes in some of the city's best scenery including nature reserves, parks, docklands and cemeteries. The vast scale of the city becomes apparent over the 15 official sections of the route. The more adventurous should try and complete it in three daily marathons.

155 SECRET ADVENTURES

+44 (0)20 3287 7986
www.secretadventures.org

This innovative small company organises several micro-scale adventures a month that are designed to generate a sense of exploration and wonder. Events include night-time kayak trips on the river to Greenwich, late night full-moon skinny dips and woodland walks with campfires. The events are a lot of fun, very sociable and a great way to meet people.

5 places for
SPORTS

---

456 HERNE HILL VELODROME

104 Burbage Road
SE24 9HE
South ⑤
www.hernehillvelodrome.com

This historic velodrome was built in 1891 and hosted the 1948 Olympics. The refurbished concrete track is 450 metres long and regularly hosts races. There are also training sessions and starter courses to take part in on the track, plus cycle polo meets and a cyclo-cross course.

457 WESTWAY SPORTS CENTRE

1 Crowthorne Road
W10 6RP
West ⑦
+44 (0)20 8969 0992
www.sports.westway.org

This varied and well-equipped sports centre has a large site underneath the A40 Westway flyover. It's run by a charity and was one of Britain's first social enterprises when it opened in 1971. Facilities include an excellent indoor climbing wall, synthetic football pitches and a gym and fitness studio.

458 MARSHALL STREET LEISURE CENTRE

15 Marshall St
W1F 7EL
Soho ①
+44 (0)20 7871 7222

Originally built in 1850 as public baths this historic site in Soho was reopened in 2010. The beautiful 1930s art deco pool has been retained along with its Sicilian marble floors and barrel-vaulted ceiling. 30 exercise classes are run weekly in the fitness and dance studios.

59 2020 ARCHERY

The Downside Centre
Coxson Place
Druid St
SE1 2EZ
Southbank ④
+44 (0)20 3130 6797
www.2020archery.co.uk

Find your range at this friendly indoor archery club near London Bridge. They offer regular Have-A-Go sessions with expert tuition for beginners as well as family sessions, weekend courses and longer training programmes. Or try Archery Tag, a safe form of 'dodgeball with arrows' which is great fun for groups to compete in.

60 QUEEN ELIZABETH OLYMPIC PARK

Stratford
Hackney ⑨
+44 (0)800 072 2110
www.queenelizabeth
olympicpark.co.uk

Opened to the public in 2014 the Olympic Park in Stratford is a sprawling site that includes housing, culture and sporting facilities, all looked over by Anish Kapoor's bizarre Tower structure. The Velo Park has an indoor velodrome and outdoor circuits. The Aquatics Centre has wonderful facilities and you can also participate in hockey, tennis, basketball and badminton here.

456 HERNE HILL VELODROME

5

QUIET PLACES

for calm and relaxation

---

461 **TIBETAN PEACE GARDEN**
GERALDINE MARY
HARMSWORTH PARK
St George's Road
SE1 6ER
Southbank ④
www.tibet-foundation.org/page/peace_garden

Opened by the Dalai Lama in 1999 this is a beautiful garden with the Kalachakra Mandala at its centre, surrounded by meditating seats, sculptures and Tibetan and Himalayan herbs and plants. Designed to promote the need for understanding between different cultures and an awareness of Buddhist culture, it shares a park with the Imperial War Museum.

462 **PHOENIX GARDEN**
21 Stacey St
WC2H 8DG
Covent Garden ①
www.thephoenixgarden.org

This small and enclosed community garden in the middle of the West End was created in 1984 on the site of a former car park. It's located behind the Phoenix Theatre and can be accessed by a number of dingy alleyways. Offering a tranquil and pleasant respite from the city the garden is full of interesting planting that's designed to encourage wildlife.

463 POSTMAN'S PARK

St Martin's Le Grand
EC1A
City ④
www.postmanspark.org.uk

This small and atmospheric park lies on the site of the former burial ground of St Botolph's Church, Aldersgate. Underneath an awning is the Watt's Memorial to Heroic Self Sacrifice, with 54 Arts and Crafts memorial tablets commemorating people who lost their lives whilst attempting to save others. It's a peaceful enclosed space with trees, a pond and a water fountain.

464 INNER SPACE

36 Shorts Gardens
WC2H 9AB
Covent Garden ①
+44 (0)20 7836 6688
www.innerspace.org.uk

Relax, recharge and refresh yourself at this meditation and personal development centre run by the Brahma Kumaris World Spiritual University. They offer a number of different regular courses in meditation as well as talks and lectures that promote inner calm. A Quiet Room is available for contemplation and reflection.

465 USHVANI

1 Cadogan Gardens
SW3 2RJ
South West ⑥
+44 (0)20 7730 2888
www.ushvani.com

This upmarket Malaysian-inspired spa in Chelsea is the perfect place for some prostrate pampering. Discreetly located on a side street, behind a heavy wooden door, lies a beautiful interior with stone baths, Malaysian artworks and wooden sculptures. Numerous massages and scrubs are available, plus a hydrotherapy pool and steam room.

CABMAN'S SHELTERS

35 RANDOM FACTS AND USEFUL DETAILS

---

5 unusual
STREET NAMES

466 **BUNHILL ROW**
East ③

Today Bunhill Row runs next to the Bunhill Fields nonconformist burial ground. The name derives from a corruption of 'bone hill'. The fenland area had been associated with internments since Roman times and was to become a depository for 1000 cartloads of bones in 1549. It formed a hill large enough to support three windmills.

467 **PETTY FRANCE**
South West ⑥

This short street in Westminster was once an area settled by French Huguenots who had migrated to escape religious persecution in the 16th century. It was noted that French was the predominant language spoken in the area, which became known as Petty France, or 'Little France'.

168 COCK LANE
City ④

Cock Lane's name derives from it being a centre for the breeding of fighting cocks in medieval times. The blood sport was very popular in the city in that time. Cock Lane was also home to a number of brothels and was the site of an infamous fraudulent haunting concerning Fanny, the Cock Lane Ghost.

169 HOUNDSDITCH
City ④

Houndsditch follows the path of a defensive ditch that ran outside a section of the Roman London Wall. The ditch was notorious as a depository for all kinds of waste, but particularly dead dogs. Several dog skeletons were disinterred here in 1989. The name Houndsditch first appears in written history in the 13th century.

170 CARDINAL CAP ALLEY
Southbank ④

This tiny, narrow alleyway runs between some historic houses near the Globe Theatre. It's thought that the name may relate to a brothel in the alley that was frequented by bishops. However, it's more likely to be a reference to Cardinal Beaufort who landed here from Rome carrying a broad-rimmed red hat. The alley has recently, and very controversially, been gated shut.

5 unusual
URBAN DETAILS

---

471 CABMEN'S SHELTERS

Thirteen of these distinctive green sheds are scattered around London's streets. They are survivals from a programme begun in 1875 to provide (horse-drawn) hansom cab drivers with shelter and food and drink. They still service taxi drivers today, providing a place for a cup of tea and a chat. The public can purchase good value refreshments from a hatch, but not enter the shelters. One can be found outside the V&A's main entrance.

472 GIRO'S GRAVE

Waterloo Place
(near 9 Carlton House
Terrace)
SW1Y
Covent Garden ①

A small tombstone under a tree marks the spot where Dr Leopold von Hoesch's Alsatian was buried in 1934. 'Ein Treuer Begleiter' – a true companion – reads the inscription. Hoesch was German Ambassador during the last days of the Weimar Republic and the beginning of the Nazi administration. This has unfairly earned poor Giro, who suffered death by accidental electrocution, the sobriquet 'the Nazi Dog.'

▽3 MARK WALLINGER'S LABYRINTH

www.art.tfl.gov.uk/labyrinth

British artist Mark Wallinger was commissioned by the London Underground to complete a major new work celebrating its 150th anniversary in 2013. Wallinger's Labyrinth consists of 270 unique pieces, one for each tube station. The complex labyrinthine black and white circular designs are an analogy for journeys through the underground system.

▽4 CLEOPATRA'S NEEDLE TIME CAPSULE

Victoria Embankment
WC2N 6PB
City ④

The needle is an Egyptian obelisk standing 22 metres high beside the Thames. It dates from 1450 BC and was relocated to London in 1878. Buried underneath it is a time capsule that offers an insight into the Victorian age. Among other things it contains cigars, a set of British coins, a baby's bottle, hairpins, tobacco pipes, daily newspapers, a portrait of Queen Victoria and photographs of the leading English beauties of the time.

▽5 ELY PLACE

EC1N 6RY
Clerkenwell ②

Ely Place is a living anachronism from medieval times, a small cul-de-sac that's technically a part of the rural county of Cambridgeshire. This administrative enclave began when the Bishops of Ely settled here in 1290. It remains the last privately owned street in London, which police need permission to enter. Ely Place is home to historic St Etheldreda's Church.

5
UNDERGROUND STATION
to visit

---

476 **CANARY WHARF**

This vast, cathedral-like station was built in 1999 and designed by Norman Foster for the Jubilee Line extension. There's little evidence of it at ground level, only discreet glass canopies at the two entrances - you need to go underground to appreciate the scale of this enormous and elegant space, excavated 24 metres deep into a former dock.

477 **PARK ROYAL**

Located at the western end of the Piccadilly Line, Park Royal station was built in 1931. The distinctive interconnecting geometric shapes of the brick and glass design are characteristic of the art deco / Streamline Moderne style. It has three receding windowed tiers with a circular ticket hall and a tall brick tower above.

78 **BARONS COURT**

Serving the District and Piccadilly lines in west London, the platforms at this modest station are actually overground and in the open air. The beautiful station building was constructed in 1906 and retains many original features including terracotta art nouveau fascia and lettering, and a green-tiled interior. The eastbound island platform features a unique wooden bench.

79 **COCKFOSTERS**

Serving the suburbs at the end of the Piccadilly Line, Cockfosters was designed in 1933 by Charles Holden, the principal architect of London Underground at the time. The station retained many of its original light and sign fittings. The exposed concrete structure of the cantilevered platform canopy is highly distinctive, and a fine example of the Modern style.

80 **WESTMINSTER**

A marvel of civic engineering, Westminster station was rebuilt for the Jubilee Line extension in 1999 to a design by Hopkins Architects. It's thrilling to descend the chain of escalators 30 metres down. Composed of exposed concrete and stainless steel beams that fly out into the air from wall to wall, it has a heady, futuristic atmosphere.

5

BLUE PLAQUE

residences

---

481 **23 AND 25 BROOK STREET**
W1K 4HA
Mayfair ⑧

Composer George Frederic Handel lived at number 25 from 1723-59, during which time he composed great works including *Water Music* and *Messiah*. Legendary rock guitarist Jimi Hendrix lived at number 23 from 1968-69. In 2016 the 'Handel and Hendrix in London' museum opened, featuring the restored period rooms of both musicians.

482 **51 GORDON SQUARE**
WC1H
Bloomsbury ②

This Bloomsbury building and its neighbouring townhouses were the central focus in the early part of the 20th century for the influential set of artists, writers and intellectual who made up the bohemian Bloomsbury Group. Virginia Woolf, Clive Bell, John Maynard Keynes and Lytton Strachey lived here and entertained other members of the influential group including Duncan Grant and Vanessa Bell.

83 **20 AND 22 FRITH STREET**

W1D 4RL
Soho ①

Child genius Wolfgang Amadeus Mozart lived, played and composed at number 20 in the years 1764-5 when he was only eight years old. Next door, at number 22, brilliant Scottish engineer John Logie Baird gave the first demonstration of television in 1926, unveiling his invention to an astounded audience including members of the Royal Institution.

84 **12 GREAT NEWPORT STREET**

WC2H 7JA
Covent Garden ①

This address was home to the former jazz club Studio 51. A blue plaque commemorates Ken Colyer, an English jazz musician who played in the basement here during the years 1950-73. Colyer grew up nearby in Soho, which was the nucleus for jazz in the UK at the time, and went on to become a successful trumpeter, cornetist and band leader.

85 **28 DEAN STREET**

W1D
Soho ①

Karl Marx, the German philosopher and revolutionary socialist who wrote *The Communist Manifesto* and *Das Kapital*, lived here with his family from 1851 to 1856 in two small upstairs rooms. During this time he subsisted on a small weekly sum given to him by Friedrich Engels. Today it's home to the Quo Vadis restaurant which has a private dining room in Marx's name.

5
CULT FILMS
set in London

---

486 PERFORMANCE

This complex gangster drama starring James Fox, Anita Pallenberg and Mick Jagger was filmed in 1968 and released in 1970. Much of the film is located and filmed in the Powis Square area of Notting Hill, where Jagger's eccentric rock musician character lives. It also features scenes in Richmond Park, Wandsworth, Fulham Road and Wigmore Street.

487 28 DAYS LATER

This 2002 post-apocalyptic horror film was directed by Danny Boyle and depicts the breakdown in society after a highly contagious virus is accidentally released. It features incredible shots of desolate, deserted London streets. Locations include Canary Wharf underground station, Westminster Bridge, Whitehall, Piccadilly Circus and The Royal Exchange.

88 LONDON

Patrick Keiller's 1994 film is a unique and brilliant work and a visual diary of the city. It follows Robinson and an unnamed narrator, neither of whom appears on screen, as they travel the capital meditating on the built environment. Locations include Vauxhall, Stockwell, Brixton Market, Docklands, Wembley, Arnold Circus, St Mary-le-Strand and the City.

89 WITHNAIL AND I

Bruce Robinson's 1987 film is set in the London of the late 1960s, and follows the fortunes of two unemployed actors who live in a squalid Camden Town flat. It features scenes filmed in Regent's Park, London Zoo, Camberwell and Notting Hill, which was the location for a memorably confrontational scene in the recently demolished Mother Black Cap pub.

90 PASSPORT TO PIMLICO

Set in Pimlico in post-war London, this classic Ealing comedy from 1949 was filmed on a set built on a real bomb site. The farcical plot centres on the discovery, in a bomb crater, of a document that proves Pimlico is in fact a part of Burgundy in France. Scenes were shot in Lambeth Road, Piccadilly Circus and London Zoo.

5
FASCINATING BOOKS
about London

---

491 NAIRN'S LONDON
Ian Nairn
Penguin
Modern Classics
1966

Recently re-published, architectural writer and critic Ian Nairn's masterpiece is a collection of observations on London buildings and districts. "A record of what has moved me between Uxbridge and Dagenham", it's an idiosyncratic and intensely subjective meditation on the city, featuring railway stations, synagogues, markets, churches, monuments, and 27 pubs. The writing is a work of literature.

492 CYCLOGEOGRAPHY
Jon Day
Notting Hill Editions
2015

Subtitled 'Journeys of a London Cycle Courier' this book is a portrait of London from the unique perspective of the saddle, and an essay about the bicycle and its role in the collective imagination. Day spent five years cycling hundreds of miles a week. Imbedded in the courier sub-culture, he was able to gain illuminating insights into the psychogeography of the city.

493 PORTOBELLO ROAD: LIVES OF A NEIGHBOURHOOD

Julian Mash
Frances Lincoln
2014

This is a fascinating portrait of one of London's most famous streets and the people who have lived there over the last 50 years. Mash combines his own experiences of working in the area with interviews of over 60 Portobello residents – market traders, film-makers, shop-keepers, punks and poets – to portray the real character of the street, its history and its people.

494 ON BRICK LANE

Rachel Lichtenstein
Penguin
2008

Brick Lane is one of east London's most fascinating and historic streets. Lichtenstein spent ten years researching its history by talking to the people who live there and the families of previous inhabitants. It's a complex and engaging story that relates the experiences of immigrant populations and the more recent arrival of artists and creatives in the area.

495 CAPITAL

John Lanchester
Faber and Faber
2012

One of the best London novels in recent years was written by a journalist who covered the 2008 financial collapse. This moral fable is set in a fictional and rapidly gentrifying Clapham street in the run up to the crisis. It's a dramatic portrayal of London's fragmentation told through the precise observation of archetypal characters – bankers, shop workers, families, asylum seekers.

5

ESSENTIAL WEBSITES

496 TRANSPORT FOR LONDON
www.tfl.gov.uk

A fantastic resource for anyone navigating a route across London by public transport. It takes into consideration all the modes of transport available and offers a range of routes to complete the journey in the quickest time possible. It's especially useful if you are travelling to or from an area that's not on the tube.

497 NTS RADIO
www.nts.live/about

Founded in 2011 and based in Dalston, NTS is London's best online radio station. Charlie Bones' morning show is a must, there are regular spots for established and obscure DJs, curated guest residencies, regular specialist music programmes and one-off shows for artists and DJs in town for gigs. It's an exciting community built by music lovers for music lovers. Their motto is 'Don't Assume.'

498 LONDONIST
www.londonist.com

This online magazine offers a broad and eclectic range of news, reviews and features about what's happening in the city. It celebrates the best London has to offer and highlights some of the more surprising and less obvious attractions, events, stories and things to do each week.

499 JUST OPENED LONDON
www.justopenedlondon.com

Just Opened lists and features the most exciting and interesting new openings in London – whether shops, restaurants, bars, clubs, galleries, events, special exhibitions or museums shows. If you need to know the very latest new thing that's happening in town then this is a great resource.

500 THE GREAT WEN
www.greatwen.com

'The Great Wen' is a disparaging nickname for London coined by William Cobbett in the 1820s, describing an overpopulated city that resembles a swollen boil. It's been appropriated by Peter Watts as the name for his engaging blog that celebrates strange and unfamiliar stories about London life, culture and history.

INDEX

COLOPHON

EDITING *and* COMPOSING – Tom Greig

GRAPHIC DESIGN – Joke Gossé and Tinne Luyten

PHOTOGRAPHY – Sam Mellish – www.sammellish.com

COVER IMAGE – Brixton Market

The addresses in this book have been selected after thorough independent
research by the author, in collaboration with Luster Publishers. The selection is
solely based on personal evaluation of the business by the author. Nothing in
this book was published in exchange for payment or benefits of any kind.

D/2016/12.005/1

ISBN 9789460581731

NUR 506

© 2016, Luster, Antwerp

Fifth edition, November 2017 – Tenth reprint, February 2018

www.lusterweb.com – www.the500hiddensecrets.com

info@lusterweb.com

Printed in Italy by Printer Trento.

FSC www.fsc.org — MIX Paper from responsible sources FSC® C015829

All rights reserved.
No part of this publication may be reproduced, stored in a retrieval system,
or transmitted, in any form or by any means, without the prior written
consent of the publisher. An exception is made for short excerpts which may
be cited for the sole purpose of reviews.